Workshop
Accessories
You Can Make

Workshop
Accessories
You Can Make

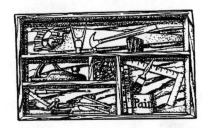

Edward A. Baldwin

TAB Books
Division of McGraw-Hill, Inc.
Blue Ridge Summit, PA 17294-0850

Cam Dog Clamps™
Cam Bar Clamps™
Bench Mate™   Edward A. Baldwin

Disclaimer
The projects contained in this book are original designs by Edward A. Baldwin. This publication is intended for your personal use and neither the designs contained herein, nor design variations, may be produced for sale nor exploited for commercial use without the written special consent of the author. No part of this publication may be reproduced, copied, or transmitted in any form. The entire contents are protected by copyright in the United States and all countries signatory to the Berne and Buenos Aires Convention. The information contained in this book is true and accurate to the best of our knowledge: however, neither the author nor the publisher can assume any responsibility for possible errors or omissions.

FIRST EDITION
FIRST PRINTING

©1993 by **TAB Books**.
TAB Books is a division of McGraw-Hill, Inc.

Library of Congress Cataloging-in-Publication Data

Baldwin, Edward A.
    Woodshop accessories you can make / by Edward A. Baldwin.
       p.   cm
    "From the 'Weekend Workshop' collections"--Added t.p.
    Includes index.
    ISBN 0-8306-2126-1   ISBN 0-8306-2124-5 (pbk.)
    1. Woodworking tools. 2. Woodwork—Equipment and supplies—Design and constructon. 3. Workshops—Equipment and supplies—Design and construction. I. Title.
TT186.B28   1993   92-34881
684'.08'028—dc20   CIP

Acquisitions editor: Kimberly Tabor
Book editor: April D. Nolan
Production team: Katherine G. Brown, Director
                Wanda S. Ditch, Layout
                Tina M. Sourbier, Coding
                Kelly S. Christman, Proofreading
                Kristine D. Lively-Helman, Indexer
                Janice Stottlemyer, Computer Illustrator
Design team: Jaclyn J. Boone, Designer
             Brian Allison, Associate Designer
Cover design:Theresa Twigg

                                                          HT1

To Don and Bobbie Anderson, two wonderful friends who know the true meaning of the words "making it." They know what it really takes to make it in today's world.

Acknowledgments

Project design: Ed Baldwin
Editorial director: Barbara Sachs Kremer
Photography: Eddie Arthur
Art: Baldwin Productions
Sawdust cleanup: Mark Baldwin
Choreographer: B. J. Stiemle

The projects in this book were made using tools supplied by
Ryobi and with router and shaper bits provided by Freud.

The projects contained in this book are but a few of the tools and accessories I have made over the years to extend the ability of my workshop to meet my needs as a woodworker. If you set your mind to it, you can make many different jigs and fixtures that will allow you to do much more in a shorter period of time—and it won't cost you a fortune.

You do not have to have a lot of woodworking tools and expensive machines to do woodworking. Many of the wood cuts and shaping necessary to build woodworking projects can be made with relatively inexpensive handheld power tools. By building your own tools and extending the capability of your power tools with various jigs and fixtures, you can do a lot of amazing things.

I have attempted to provide you with some design ideas and projects that have helped me over the years. Woodworking is a hobby for me. As long as it is fun, I will keep doing it and thinking up ways to do even more, for less money.

One of the really great rewards of working in wood is to see the eyes of little children when they are presented with a toy or that look you get from that special someone who has just received one of your projects as a gift. Another is knowing that you learned something new today, and perhaps one of the projects in this book will allow you to enjoy your woodworking hobby even more.

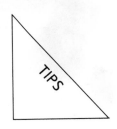

THE PROJECTS IN this book were originally built from necessity and to conserve a valuable commodity called cash. While some of the projects might look a little weird, they do work, and that is the bottom line. The construction techniques employed to build these projects are thoroughly modern and include the use of modern adhesives, current-day hardware, and both handheld and stationary power tools. As a basic premise, I used simple glue joints secured with nails or screws, or new biscuit-spline techniques strengthened with recessed nails or screws, where appropriate.

This approach might disappoint some of you who practice the time-honored techniques of traditional wood joinery and who are looking for lapped goose-neck mortise-and-tenon joints with stubbed tenons locked with V-wedges. Sorry about that. However, for those of you primarily interested in building sturdy, useful workshop accessories in a time-efficient manner, this book is going to save you money and show you some really neat ideas. Any of the projects contained herein can be modified to accommodate traditional techniques, if you so wish. Those of you who frequently construct halved, rabbeted, oblique, scarf joints will no doubt know where to put them!

Following are brief discussions of some of the various woods, chemicals, materials, and tools I used to make the projects. You will note I avoided the use of hide glue, casein glues, lacquer finishes, and the like. I opted to use the more up-to-date, easily available products that perform well and are easy to apply.

How to select wood

Walking into a home center today can sometimes be a shock when it comes to selecting wood. Most of the white woods, pine, etc., are usually not straight and perfect, but are loaded with knots and imperfections. The hardwoods, in most cases, are laminations, and they carry a hefty price. Depending on where you live, there will always be an abundance of one certain kind of wood that is generic to your area. For example, redwood might be plentiful in California, but here in the Midwest, where I live, good heart redwood is not in abundance.

Sometimes you can get a bargain by buying certain low grades of wood and ripping the boards to obtain good stock. Then, by laminating the good boards, you can make good larger stock from which to make furniture.

Getting to know someone who owns a sawmill is highly advised if you are into serious woodworking. Finding mail order houses that offer good deals on certain plywoods and hardwoods is also a good idea. If you own land with lots of trees, you can always cut your own, but it takes forever to air-dry most woods.

Generally speaking, woods are divided into two general categories: *hardwood lumber*, which comes from deciduous trees (the ones that shed their leaves every year), and *softwood lumber*, which comes from conifers (evergreens). Hardwoods are harder to cut and work with and are usually more expensive than softwoods. But, for the same reason, hardwoods make more durable and longer-lasting furniture than do softwoods.

Common hardwoods include red and white oak, walnut, pecan (which is usually hickory in disguise), ash, elm, and maple. Common softwoods include redwood, fir, cedar, and pine (both white pine, which is a soft, fine-grain wood, and yellow pine, which is almost hard enough to be considered a hardwood). Softwoods vary widely in their tendency to shrink, swell, and warp. The most stable of softwoods are redwood, pine, and cedar, but Douglas fir is also a particularly good softwood to work with.

Newly cut wood has a lot of moisture and sap; it needs to be seasoned by air- and kiln-drying. Wood that is not seasoned will warp, crack, and shrink.

When you are choosing lumber, look at the ends of the boards to check the direction of the growth rings. *Heartwood* is cut from the center of the tree and has dense growth rings. It produces a highly rot-resistant board. While heartwood might become thinner as it loses moisture, it is not as likely to crack and warp as sapwood is. *Sapwood* is cut farther from the center of the tree and is more likely to be vulnerable to rot and insect damage.

Wood grades

Lumber is graded according to the overall quality of the board. Although this brief run-down will give you an idea of the categories of wood, I think your best bet is to take your project plans to your lumber dealers, show them what you want to make, and ask if they can assist you in your selection of wood. Remember: you do not need to buy the highest grade of lumber for every project.

- *#4 Common* Low in cost and with lots of imperfections. Prone to crack (check) along the grain. Good for fences or projects where appearance is not critical.
- *#3 Common* Small knot holes are common, are easily dislodged while you work, and tend to become flying missiles when cut. Wood is prone to crack (check).
- *#2 Common* Contains some small knots, fairly clear, good for paneling and flooring and outdoor projects.
- *#1 Common* Contains some small tight knots and other insignificant imperfections; is the top grade of the regular board grades.
- *D Select* Comparable to #1 common but better seasoned and more expensive.
- *C Select* A few small blemishes on one side of the board, the other side is usually clear and almost perfect.
- *1 & 2 Clear* The best and most expensive grade of wood. Only used for the finest furniture and cabinets.

Wood joining

Wood joining is an area where fine woodworking buffs get persnickety about the proper ways of putting boards together. You really can use the simpler joining techniques combined with glues and fasteners to make the projects in this book. Mitered joints, tongue-and-grooves, or fancy dovetails are simply not necessary to build these projects. Nonetheless, the following are some common traditional joints.

Butt joints

A *butt joint* connects the end or edge of one piece to the surface, edge, or end of another. Butt joints themselves are extremely weak and need to be strengthened with splines, nails, screws, dowels, or other reinforcement. On the other hand, they are the ideal joints for putting narrow boards together to form larger boards. To minimize warps, assemble the boards with the grain of every other board inverted as shown.

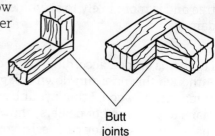

Butt joints

Rabbets

No, a *rabbet* is not a reference to a cute little bunny. In this context, it refers to a joint formed by mating pieces that provide a large area for glue, as shown. The result is a joint that is stronger than a butt joint and especially useful for cabinet, base, drawer, and box construction. This type of joint also has other uses, such as recessing the inner surface of a door inside the door opening. A rabbet joint is commonly reinforced with nails or screws.

Rabbet joints

Lap joints

A *lap joint* is used to connect two members at right angles. The two surfaces are flush and provide a large surface area for glue.

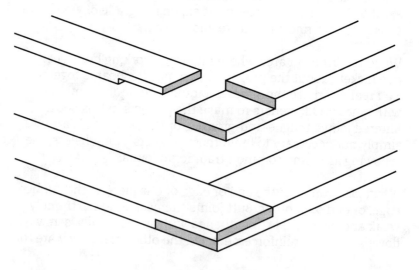

A *dado* is a groove that accommodates another member cut to
fit it. There are several kinds of dado joints. A *through dado*
extends all the way from edge to edge; a *stopped dado* extends
from one end to a point short of the opposite edge; a *blind dado*
is like a tenon and is stopped short of both edges.

Dadoes

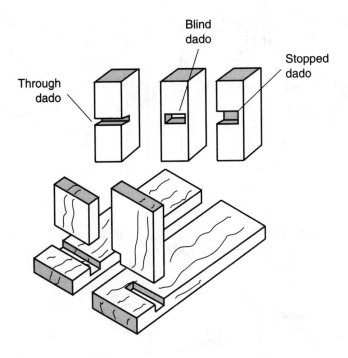

Blind
dado

Stopped
dado

Through
dado

The common garden-variety mortise-and-tenon joint is shown
at top of the next page, but there are many variations on the
basic concept of this type of joint. Mortise-and-tenon joints are
extremely tough and durable, and they can be made even
stronger with the use of wedges and pegs. An unglued joint
such as the one shown is good to use for any projects you
might want to disassemble later.

Mortise-and-tenon joints

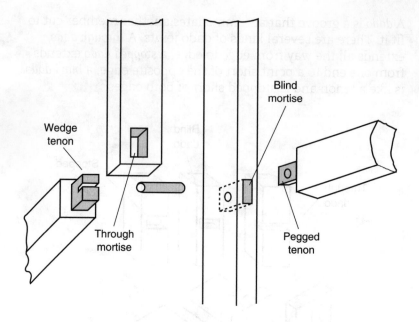

Wedge
tenon

Blind
mortise

Through
mortise

Pegged
tenon

Miters & bevels

Most picture frames contain mitered ends. Put simply, a *miter joint* connects two angle-cut ends, concealing the end grain of the wood in the process. The most common miter is a 45-degree

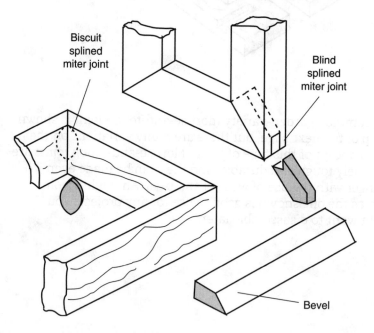

Biscuit
splined
miter joint

Blind
splined
miter joint

Bevel

xviii Workshop accessories you can make

cut, used to construct right-angle assemblies. A *flat miter* is made across the width (surface) of the board, while an *on-edge miter* is made across the end (thickness) of the board. A *bevel miter* is an angle cut made along an edge or surface.

Joints can be reinforced with the use of dowels, splines, and biscuit splines. Dowels require the use of a drill bit and a doweling jig. Regular splines are strips of wood inserted into slots or dadoes cut into the ends of wood joints, usually as a saw kerf. Biscuit splines require the use of a special biscuit slot-cutter or a router with a spiral or veining bit or slot-cutter bit.

Splines, dowels, & biscuit joinery

#0

#10

#20

Of these methods, biscuit splines are probably the most effective because the splines swell when glued into the slot and make for a tight and effective joint bindery. When used in conjunction with adhesive, recessed screws are the next choice, followed by regular splines, and then wood dowels, which are the weakest of the choices.

Splined joints may be left unglued if the assembled boards will be secured at the ends or edges. This allows for the boards in the assembly to expand and contract with changing atmospheric conditions, and it helps prevent warping and cracking.

Biscuit splines offer the most flexibility when joining wood in various positions as shown in the illustrations on this page and on page 20.

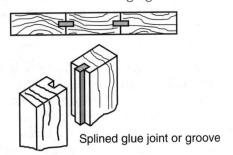

Splined glue joint or groove

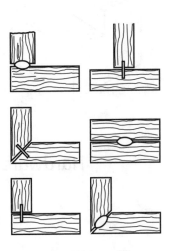

Assorted joints using biscuit splines & glue

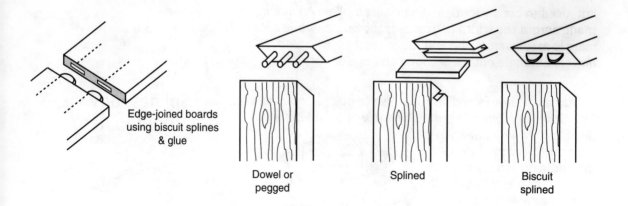

Edge-joined boards
using biscuit splines
& glue

Dowel or
pegged

Splined

Biscuit
splined

Adhesives

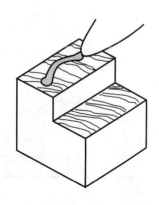

I recommend using a combination of glue and fasteners (screws, nails, bolts, dowels, splines, or biscuit splines) for all joints, unless you want to be able to disassemble the joint at a later time. *Aliphatic resin*, a cream/yellow-colored glue commonly sold as Titebond or Carpenter's glue, is best for most indoor projects. As of this writing, a new glue, "Titebond II," is being marketed as semi-waterproof, although I have not personally tested it yet in an outdoor situation. In some cases, a two-part epoxy and a clear silicone glue work best for projects designed to be used both indoors and outdoors. A marine glue and epoxy is best for most outdoor projects.

Clamping is necessary for all glued projects. When clamping, be sure the pieces are held together firmly, but so tightly that the glue is forced out of the joint. Projects that are going to get a lot of stress should be clamped overnight. While most yellow-glued projects are ready to go in about an hour, additional clamp-time is good insurance.

Hardware

All indoor projects should be made with hardware of brass, bronze, aluminum, or alloyed steel. One warning about brass screws: They usually are weak and will snap very easily, especially when used in hardwood—even with predrilled screw holes. I suggest you use the screws provided with the brass hardware with extreme caution. (Quite frankly, I usually throw them away and use brass-look-alike, alloyed-steel screws.)

Modern steel fasteners are acceptable for indoor projects. Remember, though, that all steel contains carbons, and, if the steel becomes wet or is used in a very humid condition, it deteriorates and will cause black spots to form on your project. Galvanized products are better, but galvanized coatings, too, have been known to break down and should be coated with a rust-inhibiting product. Uncoated or untreated steel hardware should never be used for outdoor projects.

Screws & nails

The kinds of screws I use for most woodworking projects are self-tapping carbon steel, either Phillips or square. For exterior projects, the best choice is Dacrotized or galvanized screws (I prefer Dacrotized). A combination screw, which combines the features of both a square and a Phillips head, is also a good choice for woodworking projects. One kind of screw you should use only with extreme caution is the old-fashioned slotted screw. Many a screwdriver has slipped off of this kind of screw and has ruined a woodworking project.

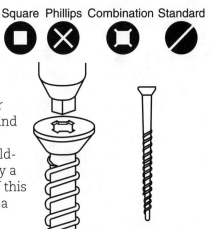

Square Phillips Combination Standard

To prevent the wood from splitting when driving screws, first drill a pilot hole for each screw—and, in some cases, for each nail. Use a drill bit slightly smaller in diameter than the screw shank.

If you are hoping to achieve a finished look, your screws should be recessed or countersunk and covered over with wood plugs. You can cut plugs that match the wood grain and blend in with your wood surface by using a plug cutter to cut them from matching wood stock. Wood plugs can also be cut from wood dowels; however, most dowels represent end grain, so your plugs will be more apparent— especially if you stain your project.

Cover screw holes with matching-grain wood plugs

Finishing nails should be toenailed or recessed below the wood surface with a larger nail or a nail set. Fill the recessed nail hole with wood filler or a paste made from sawdust and glue.

Preservatives & finishes

Preservatives are not a major consideration for most of the projects in this book. However, a good coat of varnish does add to the life expectancy of a project. Penetrating stain/sealers, such as tung oil, are good choices because they provide the convenience of staining and sealing in one application. They are available in many different tones, they enhance the grain and color of the wood, and they provide a depth of natural color you could never achieve with the flat finish of paint, which covers up the wood grain.

Hardwoods work well with stain sealers and take the chemicals rather uniformly. An excellent product for hardwoods is Danish oil stain/sealer, a resin that flows into the pores of the wood and, over time, swells—filling the wood fiber and providing a hard surface to resist water stains, food spills, etc. It is easy to apply with a rag or steel wool, and the results are quite predictable. I use this product frequently, and I have found it much faster to use than any other preservative.

If you insist on a flat finish, a top coat of a good, marine-grade varnish will do. Apply a thin first coat, and then a full-strength second coat.

Working with patterns

It is extremely difficult to write a projects book and include full-size drawings. Hence we use *scale drawings* most of the time. A scale drawing always appears on a background grid of small squares with a legend that specifies the scale. For instance, a common scale is 1 square grid on the scale equals 1 square inch.

You can copy this design to your wood one square at a time as shown on the next page, or you can use a *pantograph*, a device that can be adjusted to copy the design from the scale drawing to a full-size drawing on your wood board via a stylus and several rods that can be adjusted to various sizes. Unfortunately, most people don't own a pantograph, and copying the grid by hand is a lot of work.

The simplest and easiest way to get a full-size drawing from a scale drawing is to go to your local copy center and use their copying machine that makes enlargements. The largest-size paper these machines will use in most cases is 11"×17", but you can make as many sheets as you need to get the whole pattern, even if it is in pieces.

One final helpful hint: When you make identical parts, always use the first part you made as the pattern. This approach is especially helpful when you have to drill holes that require perfect alignment.

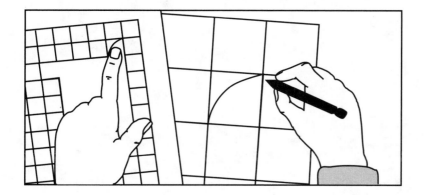

Cam dog clamps

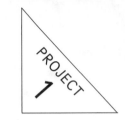

CAM DOG CLAMPS are a deviation from the old-fashioned *violin clamps*. My variation is used primarily in conjunction with bench dog holes in the top of my workbench. Cam dog clamps can be used for any situation in which you need to hold something in place while working on it, but they are particularly useful for gluing up projects. The clamps exert enough pressure to press the wood pieces together without forcing the glue out of the glue joint. Normally you position the clamps, drive them home into the bench dog hole with a hammer, and then bring the cam lever forward to exert additional pressure on the work. With the addition of a mating jaw and aluminum bar stock, you can also make bar clamps using the same techniques.

Cam dog clamps 1

Materials

(optional items are for bar clamp)

2 × 4 hardwood, oak, pecan, hickory or ash
  1 piece 2" × 10½" clamp body
  1 piece 2" × 10½" mating clamp body (optional)
  1 piece 5" × 1½" × ½" cam
  1 piece 2" × 5" wing nut wrench

Hardware & miscellaneous

1 piece 1" wood dowel 12" long
1 piece ½" wood dowel 6" long
1 piece ¼" wood dowel 1½" long
1 piece stove bolt ¼" × 2½"
1 washer
1 lock washer

1 wing nut
2 finishing nails 1½" (optional)
Carpenter's or Titebond II glue
1 piece aluminum bar stock
  ¼" × 1" × 12" (optional)
1 rivet ⅛" (optional)

Tools required

Drill with ⅛", ¼", ½" and 1" bits
Saber saw
Chisel ½"

Clamp
Hammer

Step 1

Measure and cut the clamp body pieces to size. The mating clamp body is the same size as the cam portion. If you are going to make bar clamps, cut the mating piece at this time. I would suggest that you make the cam dog clamps about 10½" to 11" long. The bar clamps need to be only about 7" to 10" long.

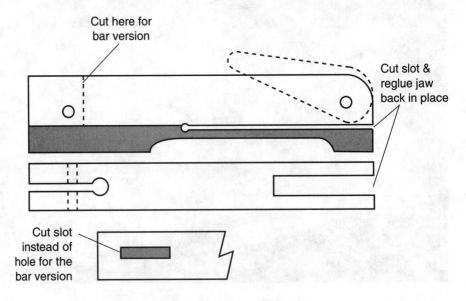

Cut here for bar version

Cut slot & reglue jaw back in place

Cut slot instead of hole for the bar version

2 Workshop accessories you can make

Cut the jaw portion of the cam clamp on the dotted line, and follow through to the front of the body. For now, ignore the hole drilled into the sides at the end of the jaw. Cut to size the slot in the front portion of the larger clamp body that will house the cam. This is an area a little wider than ½" and about 3¼" long.

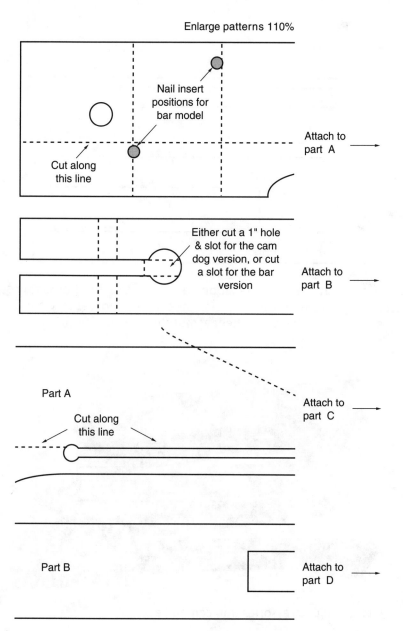

Enlarge patterns 110%

Nail insert positions for bar model

Cut along this line

Attach to part A ⟶

Either cut a 1" hole & slot for the cam dog version, or cut a slot for the bar version

Attach to part B ⟶

Part A

Attach to part C ⟶

Cut along this line

Attach to part D ⟶

Part B

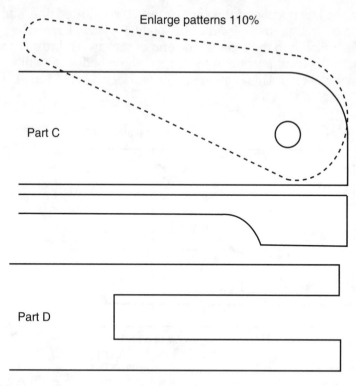

Enlarge patterns 110%

Part C

Part D

Step 3   Glue the jaw back into position and allow it to dry thoroughly before proceeding with the next step. Make another saw cut to widen the gap between the jaw and the body of the clamp.

4 Workshop accessories you can make

Drill a ¼" hole at the end of the jaw as shown. This will give the jaw the spring-action necessary for the clamping movement with the cam. If you plan to make the cam dog, drill a 1" hole at the end of the body in addition to the slot, as shown. If you plan to make the bar clamp, cut the tail of the body to size, and cut a slot for the bar by drilling successive ¼" holes and cleaning out the slot with a chisel. You want the bar to be able to move freely with no restrictions.

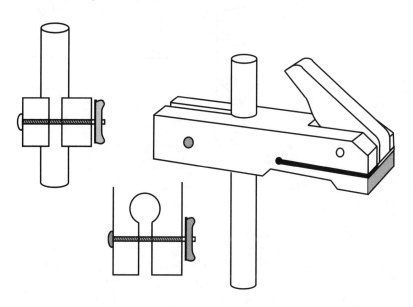

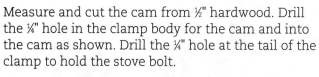

Measure and cut the cam from ½" hardwood. Drill the ¼" hole in the clamp body for the cam and into the cam as shown. Drill the ¼" hole at the tail of the clamp to hold the stove bolt.

Install the cam using a ¼" wood dowel. Bring the cam forward to see if there is enough movement of the jaw for clamping action. You should get about a ¼" to ⅜" movement. Using beeswax on the cam will make it work better.

Cam dog clamps 5

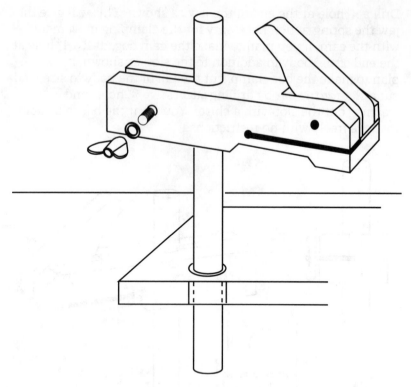

Step 6   Insert the stove bolt through the hole in the tail of the clamp and place the washer, lock washer, and wing nut in place. Insert a 12" length of 1" wood dowel and tighten the wing nut to hold the clamp in place.

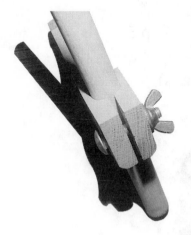

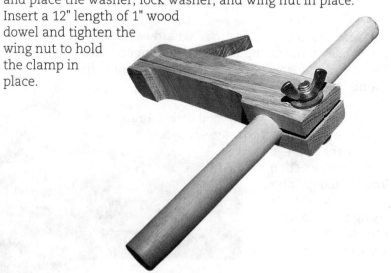

6 Workshop accessories you can make

If you are like me, you sometimes find it difficult to get a wing nut as tight as you'd like. I made this wooden wrench that allows me to add a couple of extra turns to make it as tight as I need it. This clamp is cut from 1½" × 5" hardwood with a slot in the bottom to grip the wing nut and a 6" length of ½" wood dowel at the other end, as a handle.

Making a wooden wrench

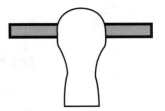

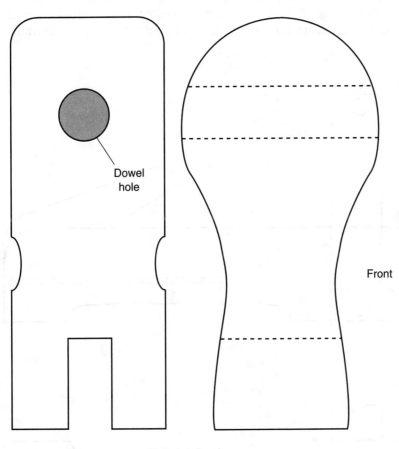

Dowel hole

Front

Full-size drawing

Step 7   I added a piece of inner tube on the jaws of the clamp for extra grip, but this is optional. The one problem with this kind of clamp is that it tends to work loose if the work receives any movement. If you want only a cam dog clamp, your job is done. If you want to make the bar clamp, read on.

Step 8   Drive two finishing nails into the end of the clamp body around the edge of the bar. This should allow the clamp to move up and down the bar, but it will also keep the clamp in position when in use. This step is crucial; the steel nails should dig into the softer aluminum bar stock and hold the clamp in position.

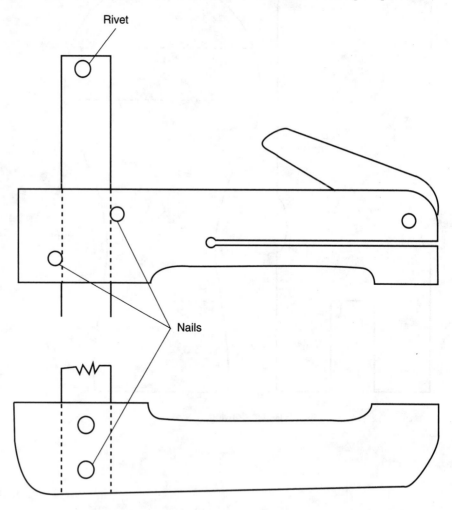

8 Workshop accessories you can make

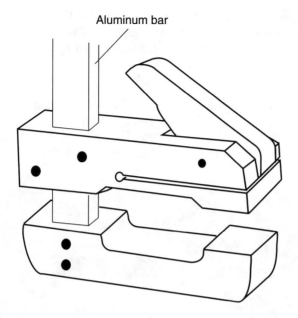

Aluminum bar

NOTE: Instead of the aluminum bar, you could use a 1" wooden dowel, as shown. In this case, it will not be difficult to get the nails to drive into the width of the dowel.

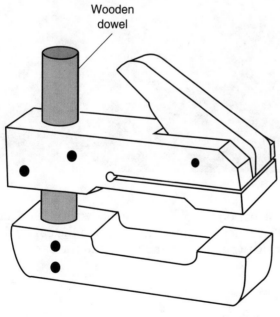

Wooden dowel

Cam dog clamps 9

Step 9 Cut the mating piece of the bar clamp body. Drill and cut the slot in the end as shown on page 3. Use a ½" drill bit and a chisel to square the sides. The bar should fit tightly in the slot in the mating clamp body.

Step 10 Drill two ⅛" holes through the end of the cam-action clamp body, and drive two finishing nails large enough to wedge into these holes and the bar stock. Cut the nails flush between the clamp body and the bar, and sand them smooth.

Position the bar on the other clamp body and drill ⅛" holes (as shown). Permanently attach the clamp to the bar by driving and wedging two nails into the holes and the bar.

Slide the cam-action clamp body over the bar, and check the jaws to make certain they are square where they meet. Drill a ⅛" hole at the end of the bar and attach a rivet so the cam action body will not fall off.

Cam bar clamps

THESE BAR CLAMPS WORK quite well for most projects that require a medium clamping action. They also provide a surface to hold the work, which is especially desirable when you are gluing up projects like door panels. The cam is extra long to provide extra leverage when applying pressure to the work. The cost of making this project is a fraction of the purchase price of an equivalent store-bought kind, and these clamps are quite simple to make. Bar clamps such as these work best if the length is kept to under 30".

Materials

2 × 4 hardwood stock, oak, ash, etc. 48" long
1 piece 1" × 1½" × 30" bar
1 piece 2" × 2¼" × 7" cam clamp body
1 piece 2" × 2¼" × 7" end clamp body
1 piece ½" × 2¼" × 7" cam lever

2 pieces ⅛" square × 2" steel bar stock
1 piece small wood peg
1 piece ¼" × 2" wood dowel
Carpenter's or Titebond II glue

Drill with ⅛", ¼" and ½" bits
Circular saw
Saber saw
Hammer
Sandpaper
Chisel ½"
Clamp
Router with rounding over bit

Measure and cut the bar to size 1" × 1½" × 30". Cut a notch in one end of the bar ½" wide and 2" deep, as shown.

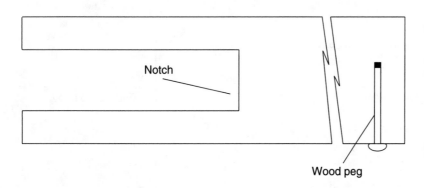

Notch

Wood peg

Using a router with a rounding-over bit, rout the edges of the board up to within ½" of the slot. Round all four edges.

Step 2 Measure and cut the forms for the cam-clamp body and the end-clamp body. Cut a rectangular hole in the end-clamp body as shown. Then drill out the center with a drill and a ½" bit, and square the sides with a chisel. You want the opening to be 1⅜ long and slightly wider than 1".

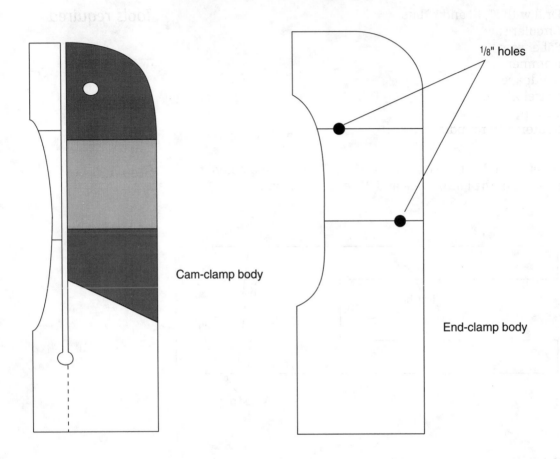

1/8" holes

Cam-clamp body

End-clamp body

Step 3 Drill two ⅛" holes through the sides of the end-clamp body as shown. Hammer the 2" lengths of ⅛" bar stock into these holes so that the clamp will dig into or grip the bar when the bar is inserted into the opening. These provide the wedging or locking action to hold the end clamp in place when pressure is applied.

14 Workshop accessories you can make

Cut the jaw portion from the cam-clamp body. Cut a ½" slot into the center of the cam-clamp body, and chisel out the recess for the bar to fit. The bar must fit snugly into this opening.

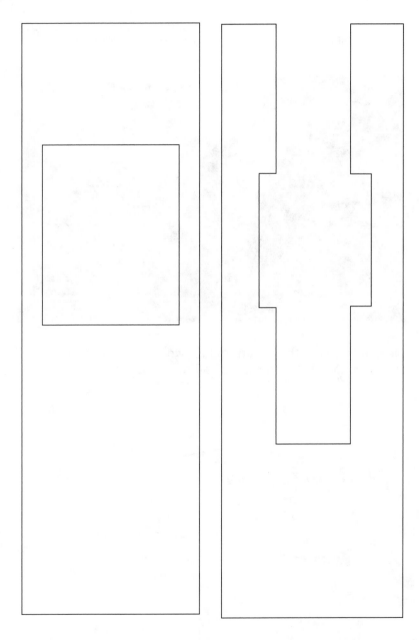

Cam bar clamps 15

Step 5   Using a drill with a ½" bit, cut out the center portion of the jaw. Square the edges with a chisel, and then glue the jaw back in place on the cam-clamp body. Clamp up the assembly, and allow it to set overnight.

Slide the cam-clamp body over the notched end of the bar and glue it in place. Clamp this assembly overnight, as well.

Step 6   Measure and cut the cam from hardwood stock. It should be slightly under 1⅛" in thickness and to the size shown.

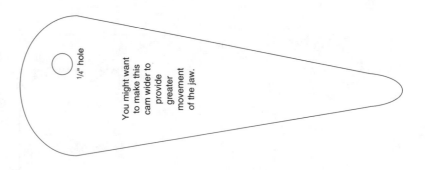

1/4" hole

You might want to make this cam wider to provide greater movement of the jaw.

Drill a ¼" hole into the top of the cam-clamp body. Insert the cam lever into the slot and position it so the lever is against the back of the jaw face. Once you are certain of the positioning, drill a ¼" hole into the lever, as well. This step is crucial. The lever must force the jaw forward approximately ⅜" to provide the proper clamping action. The lever should be able to do this with either an upward or downward movement. In other words, when the lever is horizontal to the bar, it should be just barely touching the back of the jaw.

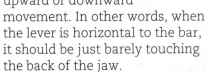

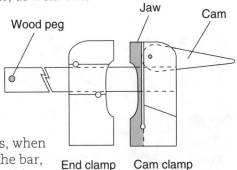

Wood peg Jaw Cam

End clamp   Cam clamp

Step 8 Slide the end-clamp body over the end of the bar and check the wedging action to make certain it is working properly. Drill a hole at the end of the bar and insert a wood peg to stop the end clamp body from falling off the bar.

Tool tote

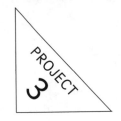
Y OU CAN CARRY a lot of different tools in this tote. The design is not new, but it is something every household should have.

The center board conveniently stores screwdrivers and chisels, while the two compartments on either side of the divider can hold hammer, nails, screws, saws, and other tools. This project takes very little skill to make and can be completed easily in one weekend.

Materials
¾" plywood or solid pine lumber
   2 pieces 9" × 12" ends
   1 piece 9" × 23" bottom
   1 piece 6" × 22½" center board
¼" plywood
   2 pieces 7" × 23½" sides

Hardware & miscellaneous
1 piece wood dowel 1" × 24" handle
14 finishing nails ¾"
6 screws drywall type 1½" long
Carpenter's or Titebond II glue
6 wood plugs ½"

Tools required
Drill with ½ and 1" spade bit and
   ½" countersink
Circular saw
Screwdriver
Hammer with nail countersink
Router with rounding-over bit (optional)
Sandpaper

Tool tote 19

Step 1 Measure and cut the two side pieces, and drill a 1" hole in the top as shown. Using a router and a rounding-over bit, rout the outside edges of the ends.

Cut a ¼" rabbet joint in the bottom of the sides as shown. NOTE: Butt joints are also acceptable.

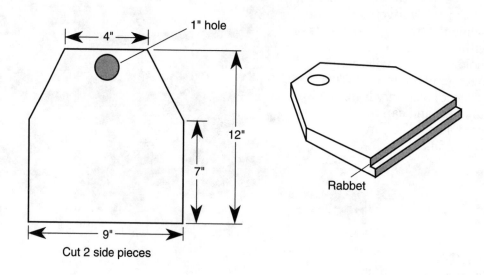

1" hole

4"

12"

7"

9"

Cut 2 side pieces

Rabbet

Step 2 Measure and cut the bottom piece. If you decide to use the rabbet joint, cut the mating ¼" rabbet in each end of the bottom piece, as shown. If you will be using a butt joint, leave the ends of the bottom piece straight.

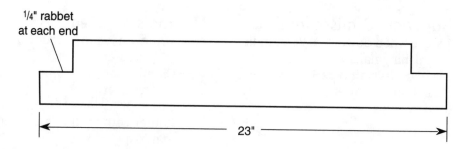

¼" rabbet
at each end

23"

20 Workshop accessories you can make

Measure and cut the center piece, and then drill ½" holes into the center of the edge of this board, spaced every 2". Measure and cut the two side pieces from the ¼" plywood; then measure and cut the 1" wood dowel to length.

Step 3

Sand the edges of all wood pieces to remove any rough edges or splinters. Gather all the pieces, and begin making a trial assembly by attaching the sides to the bottom. Next, insert the center board slightly off-center so it is not directly under the handle. Attach the handle, and add the plywood sides.

Step 4

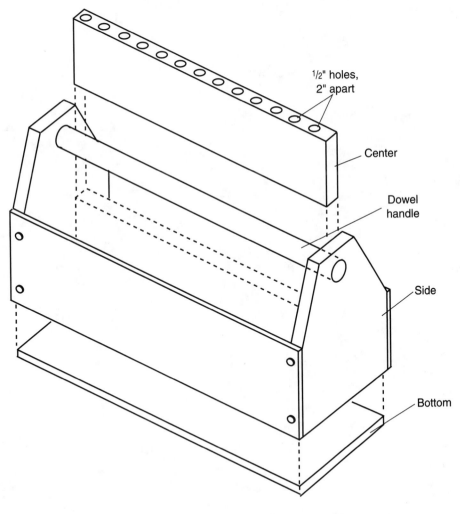

¹/₂" holes, 2" apart

Center

Dowel handle

Side

Bottom

Tool tote 21

Step 5   Use countersunk finishing nails for the sides and countersunk wood screws for the other pieces. Use glue at all joints. Countersink screws to hold the handle in place. Finally, paint the project the color of your choice.

Step tote

YOU WILL PROBABLY FIND yourself taking orders for this project because everyone will want one. It is handy in just about every room in the house. The step tote provides an extra lift for changing light bulbs or for working on other projects too high to reach, and it also contains a storage box to hide all the tools you need for fixing a screen or hanging a picture frame. This project is very practical and comes together easily in a weekend. I made my version 14" high, but you may opt to make yours a little shorter.

Materials
¾" plywood or solid wood pine
- 1 piece 11" × 16" lid
- 2 pieces 11" × 14" sides
- 2 pieces 14" × 15" front and back
- 1 piece 10¼" × 13" box floor

Hardware & miscellaneous
1 continuous hinge or
   2 small ones
20 screws drywall type 1½" long
Carpenter's or Titebond II glue
20 wood plugs ½"
Paint of your choice
1 eyescrew and hook

Tools required
Drill with ½" bit and ½" countersink
Saber saw
Circular saw
Screwdriver
Router with a rounding over bit

Step 1 Measure and cut the lid, sides, and front and back pieces from your wood stock. (NOTE: If you plan to use solid wood, the front and back pieces need to be glued up first and then cut to size.) Cut the top and bottom ends at a 5-degree bevel, as shown.

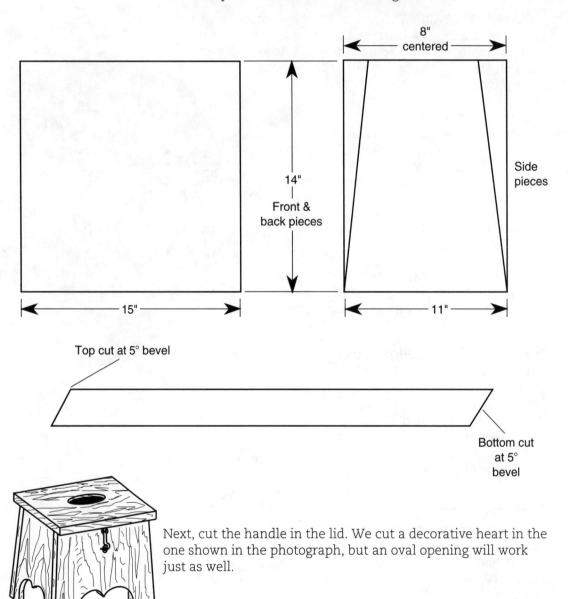

Next, cut the handle in the lid. We cut a decorative heart in the one shown in the photograph, but an oval opening will work just as well.

24 Workshop accessories you can make

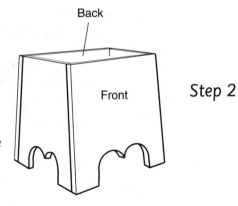

Back

Front

Assemble the front and back pieces and attach to the sides as shown. Use screws countersunk, fill the holes with wood plugs and sand the plugs flush.

Step 2

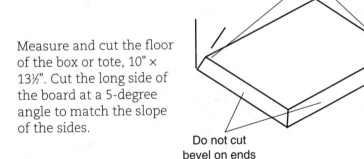

Step tote floor:
Cut at 5° bevel

Measure and cut the floor of the box or tote, 10" × 13½". Cut the long side of the board at a 5-degree angle to match the slope of the sides.

Step 3

Do not cut
bevel on ends

Drop the floor into place. Attach it using countersunk screws and glue. Fill the holes with wood plugs, and sand the floor flush with the sides.

Step 4

Step 5 Using a router with a rounding-over bit (optional), round the sides and the cutout areas, including the handle area. Turn the lid upside-down and position the step tote on top of the lid, as shown. Center the step tote on the underside of the lid, and attach the continuous hinge.

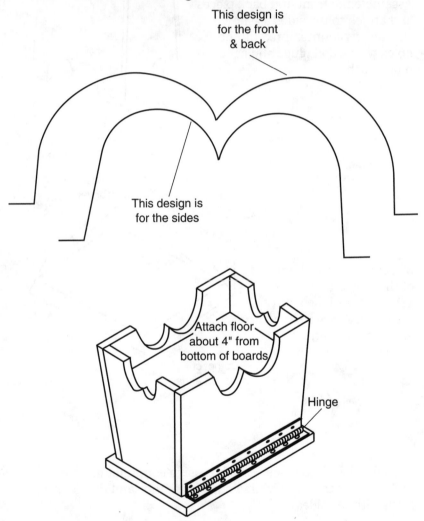

This design is for the front & back

This design is for the sides

Attach floor about 4" from bottom of boards

Hinge

Step 6 Attach the eyescrew and hook to hold the lid in place, and paint the project the color of your choice. We opted to leave the wood plain and add some decorator touches, as shown in the photograph.

Basic router bench

A ROUTER BENCH, no matter how basic, is an essential item for every workshop. I made this one from an assortment of leftovers from other projects. The top is made from a sink cutout from a kitchen improvement project, the legs and fence are scraps of wood from a toy-making project, and the polycarbonate insert that the router is attached to is leftover scrap from a ceiling skylight project. You might say that I got the router bench for free.

You can make this project with ease over a weekend—and with a minimum of expense, if you get creative in your search for materials.

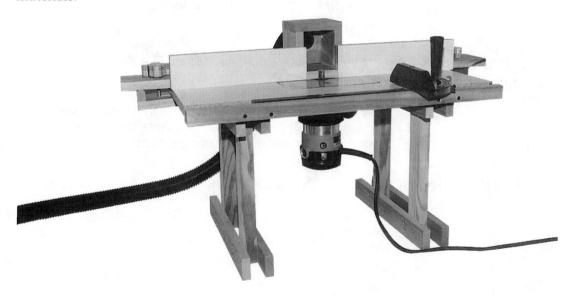

Materials

¾" laminate coated particle board 24" × 30"
  1 piece 16" × 28" router bench top
  2 pieces 3" × 13" fence faces
1 × 6 pine, fir or equivalent 14 linear feet
  8 pieces 2" × 16" top and bottom leg assembly
  1 piece ¾" × 1¼" × 28" miter gauge front board
  1 piece ¾" × 13⁄16" × 28" miter gauge slot
  2 pieces 4" × 17" fence base
  1 piece 4" × 12" fence depth of cutting adjustment board
  2 pieces 3½" × 4" fence sawdust catch sides
  1 piece 4" × 5" fence sawdust catch top
  1 piece 4½" × 5" fence sawdust catch back
  1 piece 3½" × 6" to 8" router bit safety shroud
  2 pieces 4" × 6" fence clamp bottom
  2 pieces 1" × 4" clamp rockers
  2 pieces 3" × 3" clamp handles
2 × 2 pine, fir or equivalent 6 linear feet
  4 pieces 15" long legs

Hardware & miscellaneous

1 piece Polycarbonate material (Lexan) 9" × 9" router plate
50 drywall screws 1½"
16 drywall screws 2½"
2 stove bolts ¼" × 2½" with wing nuts, washers and lock washers
2 carriage bolts ⅜" × 3½" with nuts, washers and lock washers
Titebond II or Carpenter's glue or equivalent

Tools required

Drill with countersink, ½" bit and 1¼" and 1⅜" spade or Forstner
  bits
Saber saw
Screwdriver
Circular saw
Chisel
Sander
Router with rabbeting bit
Pipe or bar clamps 20" or longer

Measure and cut the polycarbonate router base insert, 9"
square, with slightly rounded edges. If you prefer, you may
leave it square. Then measure and cut the router bench top
from a laminate-covered piece of particleboard. As you can see,
the dimensions are 16" × 28".

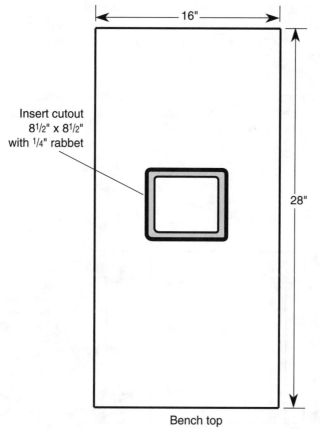

Insert cutout
8¹/₂" x 8¹/₂"
with ¹/₄" rabbet

16"

28"

Bench top

Center the polycarbonate router-
base insert on the router bench
top, and draw an outline of the
insert. Draw a matching line ¼"
wide inside the other. (This should
measure 8½" square on the inside
and 9" on the outside.) Drill a
starter hole, and cut out the inside
center of the router bench using a
saber saw.

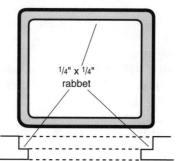

¼" x ¼"
rabbet

Basic router bench 29

Using a router with a rabbeting bit, cut a ¼"-x-¼" rabbet to the original outside line. Chisel out the corners to fit the corners of the polycarbonate insert, and drop the insert into place. Check to make certain the insert is absolutely flush with the bench top. In some cases, you might have to shim the insert, using thin wood inserts on the edges of the rabbet. This step is crucial if you want to avoid an accident or ruined work; if the insert is not flush, your work could get caught on the insert as it passes through.

Step 3   Measure and cut the wood that will form the leg assemblies, predrill the holes using a countersink, and attach the pieces with drywall screws and glue.

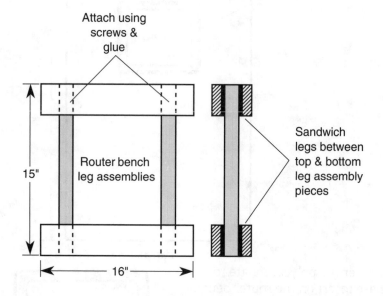

Attach using screws & glue

15"

Router bench leg assemblies

16"

Sandwich legs between top & bottom leg assembly pieces

Step 4   Attach the leg assemblies to the bottom of the router bench top as shown. Predrill the holes using a countersink and use the long drywall screws to attach. Be careful not to go though the laminate with the tip of the screw. If you want a permanent fixture, use glue also.

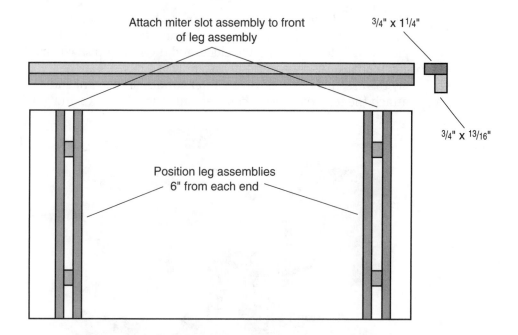

Attach miter slot assembly to front
of leg assembly

3/4" x 1¹/₄"

3/4" x ¹³/₁₆"

Position leg assemblies
6" from each end

Measure and cut the pieces forming the miter gauge slot. (You might want to alter the specifications, depending on how wide the slot must be to accommodate your own miter gauge.) Assemble the miter gauge slot assembly using screws and glue. Predrill the holes with a countersink.

Step 5

Position the miter gauge assembly and secure it using pipe or bar clamps. With a flat piece of wood, test to make certain the top edge of the assembly is perfectly even and flat with the bench top from right to left. Place your miter gauge into the slot, and check to ensure it, too, is flat with the bench top.

Mark the position of the bottom of the assembly on the front of the leg assembly. Also mark on the assembly the center position of the front of the four top leg assembly boards attached to the bottom of the bench, and remove the miter gauge assembly. Predrill holes with the counter sink in the marked positions, and reassemble with glue (repeat step 5). Once you are certain of the positioning etc., attach the miter gauge slot assembly to the front of the leg assembly pieces.

Step 6

Step 7   Measure and cut all of the pieces forming the fence per the specifications. Assemble the fence starting with the two base pieces and the sawdust catch sides, and then the top sawdust catch board. Make certain the assembly is straight. I suggest you lay the assembly face-down on a flat surface (as shown) and attach the top board using countersunk drywall screws and glue.

Step 8   Attach the back of the sawdust catch leaving slightly less than ¾" space at the bottom so that the safety shroud board will fit snugly when the assembly is clamped to the bench top. The

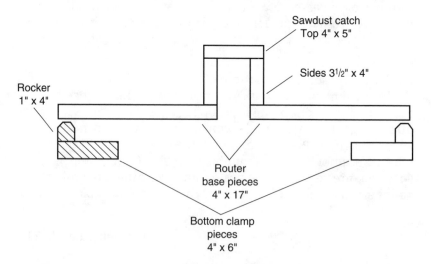

Sawdust catch
Top 4" x 5"

Sides 3¹/2" x 4"

Rocker
1" x 4"

Router
base pieces
4" x 17"

Bottom clamp
pieces
4" x 6"

cutter safety shroud is pushed into the cutter from the back until it is flush with the fence face.

Create two slots by drilling two holes, 2" apart, in a straight line on the depth-of-cut fence adjustment board. Cut out the excess between the two holes using a chisel.

Step 9

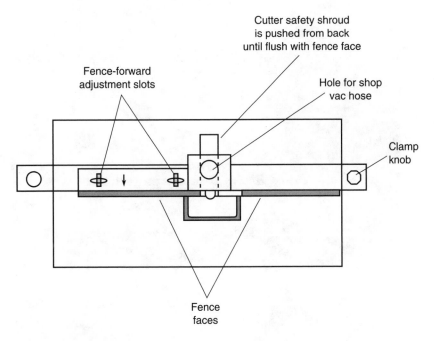

Cutter safety shroud
is pushed from back
until flush with fence face

Fence-forward
adjustment slots

Hole for shop
vac hose

Clamp
knob

Fence
faces

Position the above board on the top of the left fence base board so that it is flush against the side of the sawdust catch and the base boards. Glue the left fence face board in place on the depth-of-cut adjustment board only, as shown, using glue and clamps. Allow it to dry thoroughly before using. Do the same with the right side face, but glue it to the base and the front of the right side sawdust catch board.

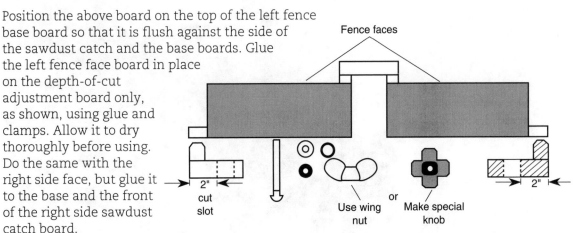

Fence faces

2"
cut
slot

Use wing
nut

or

Make special
knob

2"

Basic router bench 33

Step 10 Drill a hole through the front of each of the depth-of-cut adjustment board slots and into the base board. Turn the fence upside-down, and drill a recess for the bolt head to fit through so that it does not mar or catch on the bench top when you slide it around. Attach the depth-of-cut adjustment board to the left-hand base with bolts, washers, lock washers, and wing nuts.

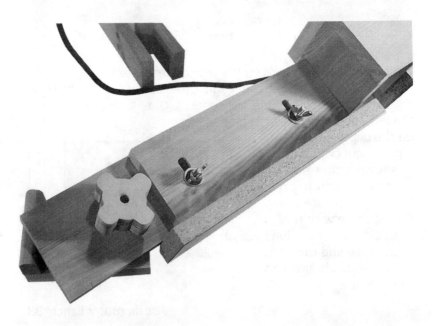

Round the two rocker boards, and attach them with glue and countersunk screws to the bottom clamp board. Place this assembly on the end of each base, and center and drill a ½" hole through both the end of the base and the bottom board. Create a slot in the base that will allow you to bring the bottom boards in about 1" when needed. In other words, drill two holes about 1" apart and chisel out the recess. Attach the bottom boards to the end boards using ⅜" carriage bolts with washers, lock washers, and wing nuts.

Step 11

For the ability to turn more pressure, make some knobs to replace the wing nuts. Drill a ½ hole in the center. Chisel out the center about ¼", and embed a nut in the recess with epoxy. This will give you greater gripping ability and allow you to lock the fence more securely to the bench top.

Making knobs to replace the wing nuts

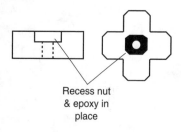

Recess nut & epoxy in place

Drill a hole in the top or back of the sawdust control boards to fit the size of your shop vac. The fence should now be ready to attach to the bench top.

Step 12

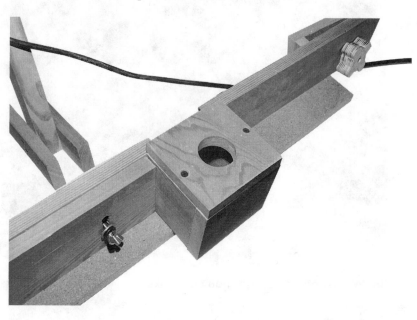

Step 13   Remove the bottom plate from the router you intend to mount on the polycarbonate insert. Using the router bottom plate as a template, mark the location of the screws that held the plate to the router. Drill recessed holes to hold the same screws that held the router plate to the router.

You will probably find one of two types of screws—either those with tapered heads, such as stove bolts, or those with flat heads. In the case of a tapered-head screw, a countersink should do the job. In the case of the flat-head screw, however, you will want to use a spade bit slightly wider than the screw head. NOTE: This step is crucial, and you need to use stops to make certain the drill bits do not go any deeper than you want them to.

Step 14   Find the dead center of the insert. The best way to do this is to first mount the router on the insert. Next, remove the router motor from the casing, and insert a tapered bit into the chuck. Place the router back into the casing, turn on the motor, and slowly lower it into the insert, cutting the center hole. Do not go all the way through; simply make a tiny opening.

36 Workshop accessories you can make

Remove the router from the insert. At this point, you have to decide if you simply want an opening in the insert for a router bit or if you also want a router bushing to use for inlay, dovetail, and template work. If you want just an opening, drill a 1½" hole in the center of the insert, and reattach the router. If you want the router bushing, proceed with step 15.

Step 15

I used a standard router bushing (made by Porter Cable) that is representative of the sizes most commonly used where I live.

Step 16

First drill a 1⅜" hole the depth of the thickness of the lip of the bushing or a little under ⅛" deep in the dead center of the insert. Next, drill a hole through the center, 1¼", and reattach the router (make certain the router is unplugged). Attach a bushing in the insert, and check the accuracy of the

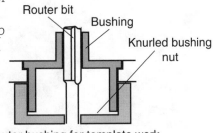

Router bit

Bushing

Knurled bushing nut

Router bushing for template work

dead-center hole by inserting a veining bit in the router chuck and lowering it into the opening in the bushing, checking to make certain the bit is dead center and not touching the sides or the center of the router bushing.

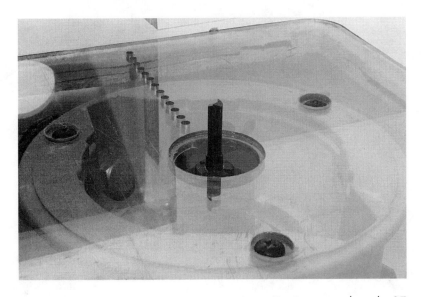

Basic router bench 37

Step 17

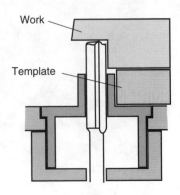

Work

Template

Place the router and insert into the opening of the router bench top. Attach the fence and the end of the shop vac hose and you are ready to make lots of fun things.

When not using the insert, make certain the shroud board is in place and flush with the face of the fence. Clamp the fence securely to hold the shroud in place.

The slider saw jig

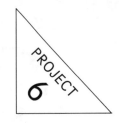

THIS PROJECT IS DESIGNED to turn your ordinary, handheld circular saw into a tool that has many of the combined characteristics of a cutoff saw, radial-arm saw, and table saw. It uses an ordinary handheld circular saw mounted on a polycarbonate sheet that slides on L-shaped rails. You can cross-cut wood up to 1¾" thick and about 46" to 48" wide. Also, you can rip any board up to 9" in width and unlimited length. Depending on the modifications you want to make to your version—and your options are many—this basic design concept will provide an amazing extension to your circular saw's capability. I call this project a "slider jig," although "a poor man's bench saw" is perhaps more appropriate.

Materials
¾" plywood exterior grade 2 × 6
  1 piece 18" × 54" table surface
  2 pieces 2" × 53½" base support
  2 pieces 2" × 10" base cross supports
1" oak or pine
  2 pieces ¾" × 1" × 54" saw supports
  1 piece 2" × 18" fence
  4 pieces 2" × 2" braces
  2 pieces 5" × 11" end saw supports
  1 piece 1½" × 2" fence separator
  1 piece 2" × 7" fence lock board

Tools required
Circular saw
Router with a ¾" straight bit
Saber saw
Drill with countersink and ¾" and ⅜" bit

Hardware & miscellaneous
1 piece wood dowel ¾" × 2"
4 pieces plywood ¼" × 1" × 5"
2 pieces aluminum ¾" angle bars 54" long
16 drywall screws 1¼"
Carpenter's or Titebond glue
1 carriage bolt ⅜" × 3" with washer and
  wing nut
3 stove bolts ¼" × 1" with nuts, washers
  and lock
  washers
Small piece sandpaper
1 piece polycarbonate material ¼" × 10" × 12"

Chisel ⅜"
Hacksaw
Screwdriver

Step 1 Measure and cut the large plywood board that will form the base or top of the table of the slider jig. Round the edges slightly to minimize any sharp edges.

Measure and cut the end boards that form the U-shaped supports for the L-angle bars. Cut a ¾" dado into the center of the board, ⅜" deep, using a router and straight bit.

Measure and cut the pieces forming the base of the saw table: two long boards and two short cross-support boards.

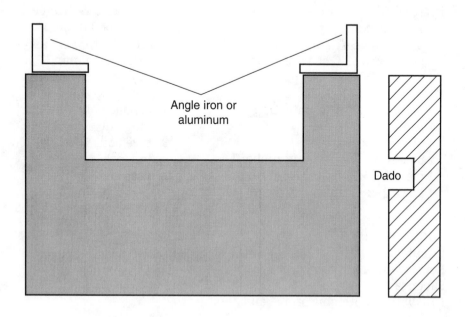

18"

10"

54"

Center-basic table frame & underside supports

Angle iron or aluminum

Dado

Assemble the boards you cut in step 1, and center them on the bottom and ends of the table board. Glue and countersink-screw them into position, as shown on page 40. NOTE: This step must be done so that the end boards are in perfect alignment and square to the table top.

Step 2

Using a router with a ¾" straight bit set to a depth of ⅜", rout three straight dadoes or slots into the top of the table as shown. These slots must be square to the table and straight. They must be exactly 10" apart from the center slot, and they must measure the same at both the front and back of the table top. The slots serve as a riding groove for a strange kind of fence I will describe in later steps.

Dado slots exactly 10" apart

Step 3

Ends must be equal in spacing

Measure and cut the two long boards forming the support for the L-angle bars. Cut a ⅜" slot, ¾" wide, the length of the boards. NOTE: These boards serve as a support to the L-angle bar to minimize sagging in the center. If you opt to use steel instead of aluminum, this step might not be necessary.

Step 4

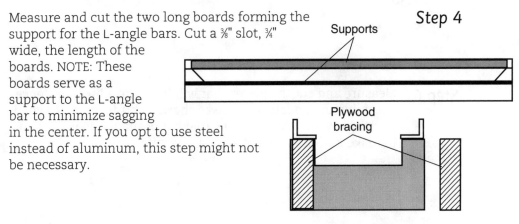

Supports

Plywood bracing

The slider saw jig 41

Step 5 Attach the wood support strips and the angle boards to the tops of the end pieces. Use countersunk screws in the ends of the angle bars. NOTE: This step must be done with precision. The bars must be evenly spaced, and the measurement of the distance between the bars at each end must be exact.

Support aluminum with wood strip

Add a small triangle of support at the inside edge of each of the end pieces. Add a strip of ¼" plywood as a support block to the outside ends of the end pieces, as shown. Attach these items using countersunk screws and glue.

Step 6 Measure and cut the pieces that will form the adjustable fence. Assemble the underside piece as shown. This fence is designed to clamp to the tabletop in a variety of positions, enabling you to make a wide variety of angled saw cuts.

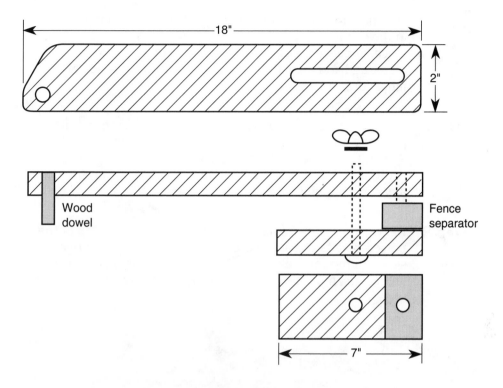

Wood dowel

Fence separator

The top of the fence must have a slot cut at one end so that the bottom assembly can slide forward and backward as the fence is moved into various positions. Use a drill with a ⅜" bit to cut the slot. Then use a chisel to cut the excess and to square the slot walls.

Center and drill a ⅜" hole in the bottom assembly for the carriage bolt. Drill a ⅜" hole in the center end of the bottom

The slider saw jig 43

assembly to hold a short length of ⅜" wood dowel that will slide in the slot in the top of the fence. Drill a ½" hole in the tip of the fence, and insert a 1½" piece of ½" wood dowel. Glue this in place, and add a small finishing nail through the side of the fence for insurance.

Step 7 Measure and cut the polycarbonate material so that it fits perfectly into the slot formed by the L-angle bar assemblies. Slide it the length of the bars to ensure that it is the proper width and that there is neither any right-to-left movement nor any spot that will catch or impede movement.

Step 8 Next, attach the circular saw of your choice to the top of the polycarbonate or base sheet. This step must be done right. Be sure you mount the saw so that it slides along on top of the angle bars, mounted on the base in a perfectly straight line.

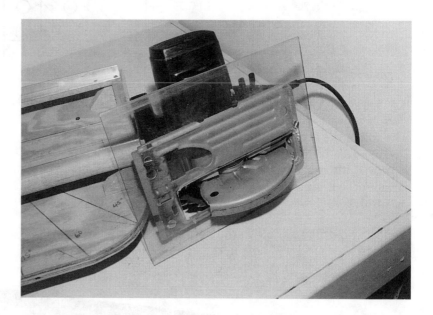

This sliding jig was built to use a standard 7½" or ¼" circular saw. I used an older-model Black and Decker that had a base plate of 5½" × 10¼".

44 Workshop accessories you can make

Start by raising the blade of the saw so that the base will fit flat on top of the polycarbonate base material. Center the saw to the front and back of the base. Move the saw to the right so that the blade is about 2" from the right edge of the base. Using a pencil, mark the outline of the saw base plate on the polycarbonate. Mark also the inside edges of the base plate where the blade and the guard will protrude.

Remove the saw from the polycarbonate, and cut the opening for the saw blade and guard—using a drill to make a starter hole and a saber saw to cut the opening. Widen the opening by a fraction of an inch so that there will be plenty of freedom of movement of the guard at both a straight and compound cut.

Step 9

NOTE: At this juncture, you have an option to cut an opening just wide enough for the saw blade to protrude and keep the guard raised. This will enable you to cut both forward, like a table saw, or backward, like a radial-arm saw. Personally, I do not like the idea of an exposed saw blade, even if it is under a protective cover, so I opted to let the guard come down as it was intended.

Use the forward hole as a pivot.
Use the left hole tp position the saw square

Use a bolt in this hole to lock the saw in position

Sand the inside and outside edges of the polycarbonate material, slightly rounding the edges. Position the saw on top of the polycarbonate base. Center it as before, and lower the saw blade and guard to see that there is adequate clearance through the opening. Clamp the saw to the base. Mark a center position at the front of the saw base plate and one to the left rear. Drill a ¼" hole through both the base plate and polycarbonate material. Unclamp the saw.

Step 10

Step 11 Widen the hole in the left rear of the saw by about ½". Attach two ¼"-×-1" stove bolts to fasten the saw to the base. The heads of the bolts must be under the base, with the threads sticking up through the saw base plate. Square the saw blade to the edge of the polycarbonate base and tighten the bolts.

Step 12 Place the saw base assembly onto the slider jig and in the tracks of the angle bars. Position the assembly to the rear. Slowly lower the saw blade so that it touches the tabletop, then lower the blade an additional ⅛." Lift the saw assembly slightly so the blade clears the table, turn on the motor, and lower the saw blade into the tabletop to make a notch. Stop the motor, and raise the saw blade ⅛".

Now move the saw blade forward and measure the distance from the right of the saw blade to the right edge of the table. If the blade is set square, the distance at the rear of the table should be the same as the front of the table. Another way to check this is to draw a straight line from the edge of the slot to the front of the table, and track the blade along this line. If any adjustment is necessary, loosen the left rear bolt and move the saw to the right or left until it tracks properly. (NOTE: This step is crucial, so be sure you do it carefully.).

Once the saw is tracking straight, tighten the bolts securely. Drill an additional hole to the right rear of the base plate and base assembly, and attach a third bolt securely. Use washers and lock washers. In my example, I had the pivot hole in the rear with the two bolts to the front of the saw—but either way will work.

Step 13

Reattach the saw to the slider jig and lower the blade to cut a ⅛" slot the length of the jig. This will be your tracking slot to make certain the saw is always square to the table top.

Drill three or more evenly spaced ½" holes along the center of the tabletop, to the left of the slot by about 1". This will allow the fence to move to various positions to accommodate a variety of board widths. Pick a spot close to the end of the table that will become your common ground for most board cuttings, and attach the fence.

Step 14

The slider saw jig 47

Step 15   Using a square, miter square, and a moveable or adjustable miter square, position the fence at 90°, 75°, 60°, 45° and 221.2° degree positions. Make absolutely certain the fence is tight at each of these positions as you mark them with a pencil line on the tabletop. Make the lines strong and visible. I suggest you position the fence at the 90° position first, cut a board to make certain the edge of the board is square, and then proceed with the rest of the markings.

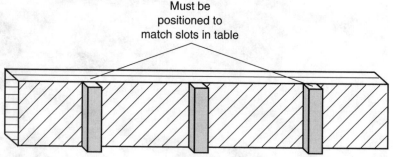

Optional second fence   I made another fence that fits into the three slots cut into the tabletop. It is positioned so that wood can be ripped to various widths. To operate it, I placed strips of ⅜"-×-⅜"-×-4" wood into the slots and positioned the fence on top. I squared the fence to the top and to the saw slot, then clamped and glued the fence into position on top of the strips of wood. When the glue dried, I added small screws (countersunk from the bottom) through the small strips into the fence. In order for the fence to work properly it must be clamped to the tabletop. Also, for better gripping action, add some sandpaper to the fence, as shown.

Must be
positioned to
match slots in table

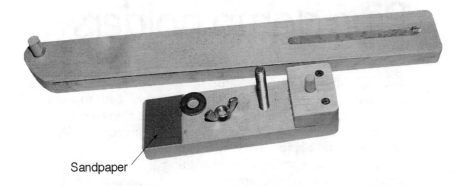

Sandpaper

I suggest you seal the table top and other wood pieces with a
tung-oil product to slightly harden the surface. You now
possess a tool that will allow you to make a wide variety of saw
cuts, and you have substantially expanded your saw's
capability.

Step 16

Pipe clamp holders

THESE SIMPLE-TO-MAKE clamp holders can really speed up a pipe-clamping operation. Pipe clamps always seem to want to flip over on their sides just when you are reaching a critical moment in the clamping operation. These projects, designed for both ½" and ¾" pipe, are very inexpensive to make and do an excellent job of holding the pipe clamps right where you want them.

Materials
½" baltic birch plywood 1 square foot
    2 pieces 2 ¼" × 3" for each clamp
2 × 4 scraps 14"
    1 piece 2¼" × 3" for each clamp

Hardware & miscellaneous
1 Tee-nut ¼" plus matching thumb screw for each ¾" clamp
1 Tee-nut ³⁄₁₆" plus matching thumb screw for each ½" clamp
Titebond or Carpenter's glue

Tools required
Coping saw
Hand saw
Drill with ¼" and ⁹⁄₃₂" bits
Sandpaper
C-Clamp

Cut the Baltic birch into strips 3" wide and 12" long. Double the strips up, and glue and clamp them to form a 1"-thick piece of wood. (This will be for the ½" clamps. The 2 × 4 stock is for the ¾" clamp.)

Step 1

When the glue has dried, cut the clamp pieces to size using the full-size drawings as a guide. Using a coping saw, cut the opening at the top of the clamp board for the size of pipe clamp you wish to make.

Step 2

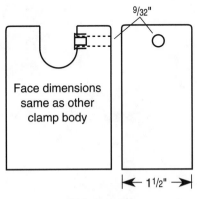

9/32"

Face dimensions
same as other
clamp body

← 1½" →

¾" pipe clamp
(Enlarge pattern 200%)

1/4

3"

← 2¼" →

←1"→

1/4"

½" pipe clamps
(Enlarge pattern 200%)

Drill a hole into the side of the clamp board as shown. Use a ¼" bit for the ½" pipe clamps, and a 9/32" bit for the ¾" pipe clamps. Drill the hole at a slight angle for the smaller clamp and straight for the larger clamp.

Step 3

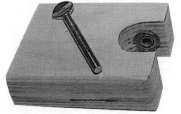

Place the appropriate-sized tee nut into the hole from the inside and pull into the wood using a C-clamp as a vice. Tighten the clamp until the tee nut sinks into the hole and the spurs dig into the wood. Make certain the inside face of the tee nut is flat against the inside wall of the clamp when you are through.

Step 4

Step 5   Sand off all of the rough edges and try them out by inserting the appropriate thumb screw through the side and into the tee nut. You do not want to apply a lot of pressure, just enough to hold the pipe into position. Too much pressure will force the pipe out of the clamp. NOTE: if you cannot find thumb screws, eye bolts will do just as well.

Homemade web clamp

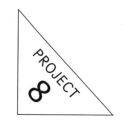

YOU CAN MAKE this project over a weekend—and for pennies compared to the store-bought kind. It can be made from found materials and an old turnbuckle (or a new one that you can purchase at a home center or hardware store). The web itself is nothing more than nylon belt material, which is available at all fabric stores. You can use your web clamp to clamp a wide variety of shapes, including hexagons, squares, and—with a slight adaption—even circles.

Materials
2 × 4 scraps cut to size
    4 pieces 1" × 1½" × 2" tenon
    4 pieces 1" × 1½" × 2" slot
⅛" plywood scraps
    8 pieces 1⅛" × 1⅛" web holders
    8 pieces 1⅛" × 2" web & project holders

Hardware & miscellaneous
4 pieces wood dowel ¼" × 1½"
1 turnbuckle 3" to 4"
1 nylon web 1" × 96"
2 belt rings 1¼"
4 small rivets with 2 washers each
Wood glue

Tools required
Saber saw
Drill with ¼" bit
Rasp or file
Clamps
Rivet tool or gun
Awl or ice pick

Step 1   Measure and cut the tenon and slot pieces to form, as shown. With a rasp or file, round over the tongue of the tenon pieces and the front of the slot pieces.

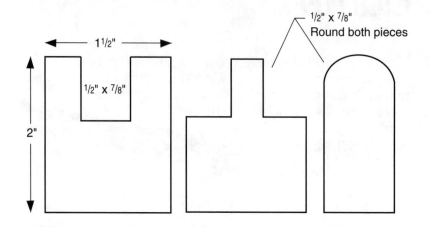

1/2" x 7/8"
Round both pieces

1 1/2"

1/2" x 7/8"

2"

Step 2   Place the tenon and mating slot pieces together and position the assembly so it can turn freely. Drill a ¼" hole through the ends of the slot piece and through the tenon of the tenon piece. Make absolutely certain that the pieces are centered.

Step 3   Measure and cut a ¼" wood dowel 1½" long. Insert the wood dowel into the mated pieces (from step 2), and make certain they still turn freely. Glue the wood dowel into the outside edges of the slot piece. Do not allow any glue to reach to the tenon piece. It is important that the dowel can still turn freely in the tenon.

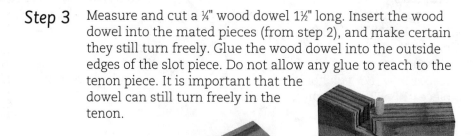

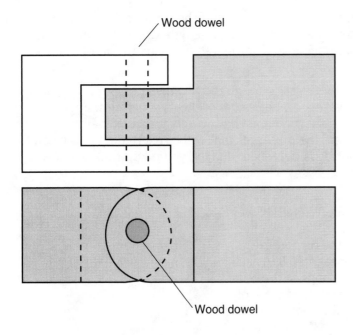

Wood dowel

Wood dowel

Measure and cut the ⅛" plywood scraps that will hold the web in place as well as the underside of the project. Position the plywood pieces as shown, and glue them in place. NOTE: You want to have about a ⅛" lip on one side to hold the web in place while applying pressure.

Step 4

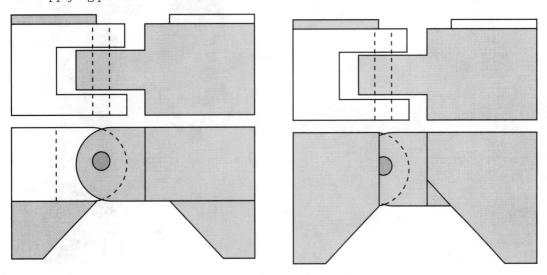

Homemade web clamp 55

Step 5   Insert the web into one side of the turnbuckle, and bend it back on itself by at least 1" or 2" of length. Create two holes through the two thicknesses of the web using an awl or an ice pick.

Step 6   Attach two rivets through the two thicknesses of web, using a small washer on both sides of the rivet before snapping it into position. The web must be securely locked or clamped to withstand the pressures that will be exerted upon it when the turnbuckle is tightened. (In fact, you might find you need 4 rivets.)

Step 7   Cut a short length of web and place it at the other end of the turnbuckle and repeat step 5. Attach the belt loops at the other end of the short piece of web and repeat step 6. You can clamp the web into position by passing it through the belt loops and then back upon itself. When pressure is applied, the web will stay in place.

Attach the clamp mechanism to a project and draw the web as tight as you can. Turn the turnbuckle to bring the two ends of the web closer together thus applying the pressure needed to clamp the project securely.

Basic web clamp

Variation

You can make a variation of the basic web clamp if you want a project that is a tad bit easier to use. This version is made from ½" scrap wood Baltic birch plywood that is laminated into a U shape. The clamp uses one eye bolt, through which the web is

Variation

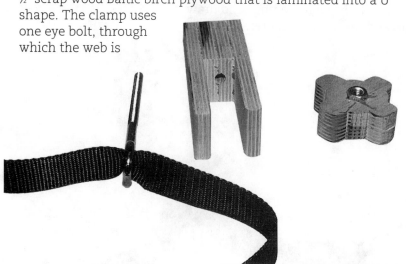

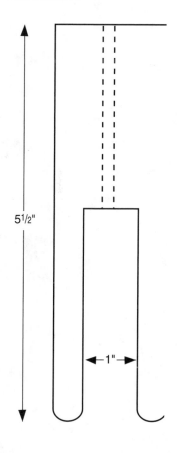

5½"

◄—1"—►

Homemade web clamp 57

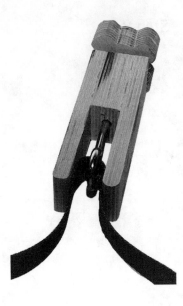

passed. As you tighten the eye bolt, the web tightens around the project.

I used epoxy to embed a nut in a small wooden knob to make it easier to turn and draw the eyebolt tight.

Glue strips of ⅛" plywood to the sides to prevent the U lips from pulling apart as tension is applied.

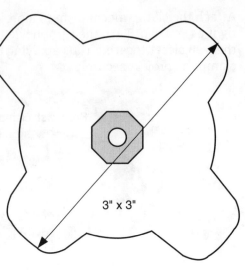

3" x 3"

In this example, it is only necessary to have the two belt rings at one end of the web because the device for applying the pressure can be placed anywhere along the web. Put one end of the web through the rings and draw it tight, then use the device to add the additional pressure.

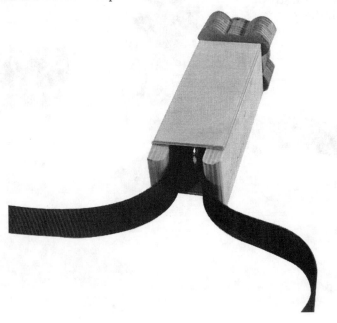

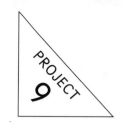

The ultimate router bench

THIS PROJECT ALLOWS you to use two routers for different applications. It has an assortment of miter gauges and fences that make it a very versatile tool indeed. The drawer can contain your router bits and wrenches, as well as other necessary parts. The fence has provisions for stops and other accessories to enable you to shape and rout curved work. If you are handy with electrical wiring, you can also rig a router on/off switch for ease of operation.

I used laminated particleboard from sink cutouts for the sides and top of this project as well as for the fence. You can substitute plywood, but I recommend a laminate for the top surface at least. I also used walnut strips for the side trim, to provide a contrast against the white laminate.

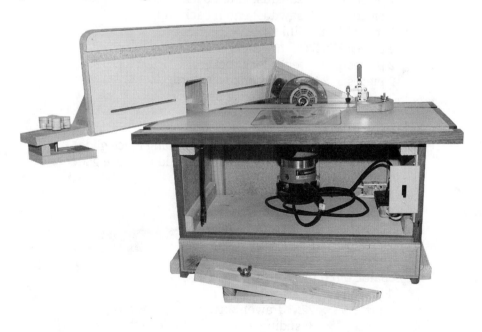

The ultimate router bench 59

Materials

¾" laminated particleboard 10 square feet
2 pieces 13" × 14½" sides
2 pieces 13" × 9" back
2 pieces 13" × 2¼" inside back sides
1 piece 13" × 3½" inside back
1 piece 16" × 28" top
2 pieces 3" × 3½" stops
1 piece 9" × 27" fence facing
1 piece 7" × 13" sliding fence face

2 × 4 white pine stock 5 linear feet
2 pieces 14½" × 2½" feet or runners
2 pieces 1½" square × 13" inside back supports

1 × 4 white pine scrap 12 linear feet
2 pieces 1½" × 12" shelf support
2 pieces 2¼" × 9½" drawer sides
1 piece 2¼" × 20¾" drawer back
1 piece 2¼" × 22⅜" drawer front
2 pieces 3" × 17" fence bottom back
2 pieces 3" × 3" fence back supports
2 pieces 3" × 3¼" sawdust catch sides
1 piece 3" × 5½" sawdust catch top
1 piece 4" × 5½" sawdust catch back
1 piece 1" × 5½" sawdust catch back support
1 piece 3" × 8" mini fence
2 pieces 3" × 5½" fence lock
2 pieces 1" × 3" fence lock rocker
2 pieces 3" × 3" sliding fence supports
2 pieces 3" × 3" sliding fence back

1 × 8 oak 4 linear feet
2 pieces 4" × 6" miter gauge
2 pieces 1" × ⅜" 11" miter gauge & sliding fence glide
2 pieces 1½" × ⅜" 11" miter gauge & sliding fence glide

¾" × ¾" walnut 10 linear feet
2 pieces 13" table back trim
2 pieces 16¾" table side trim
1 piece 29½" table front trim
2 pieces 14" front facing
1 piece ½" × 22½" shelf facing

½" Baltic birch plywood
1 piece 11¾" × 22½" shelf
1 piece 9½" × 22⅜" drawer bottom
1 piece 7" × 13" sliding fence adjustable face

60 *Workshop accessories you can make*

1 piece polycarbonate 8½" × 8½" router plate
1 piece polycarbonate 11" × 12" back router plate
1 piece polycarbonate 3" × 5" sliding fence window
2 carriage bolts ⅜" × 3" with wing nuts and washers fence lock
2 flat headed slotted stove bolts
¼" × 2" with washers and wing nuts miter gauge locks
2 flat headed slotted stove bolts
2" × ⅛" with wing nuts and washers for stops
30 finishing nail 1½"
30 drywall screws 1¼"
Wood filler
Threaded insert for a ¼" machine screw with matching washer
and wing nut

Drill with ½" bit and countersink router with rounding-over and
    dovetail bits and ½" straight bit with bottom bearing
Hammer
Screwdriver
Saber saw
Circular saw

Measure and cut the pieces forming the sides, back, and feet of
the router bench. The feet should have a dado or groove cut the
length of the feet, 1½" wide and ¼" deep.

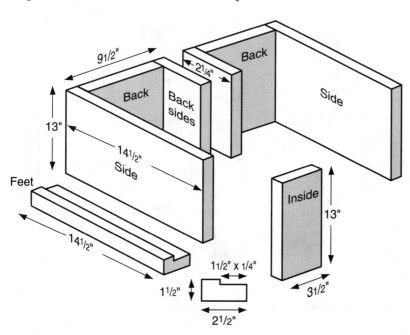

Step 2   Glue the pieces and clamp them in the position shown. Allow this assembly to dry before proceeding. Measure and cut the braces and glue in position as shown, using screws to hold them in position.

Step 3   Attach the feet as shown, using glue and screws. There should be a ¾" lip on the inside of the assembly for the drawer to glide on.

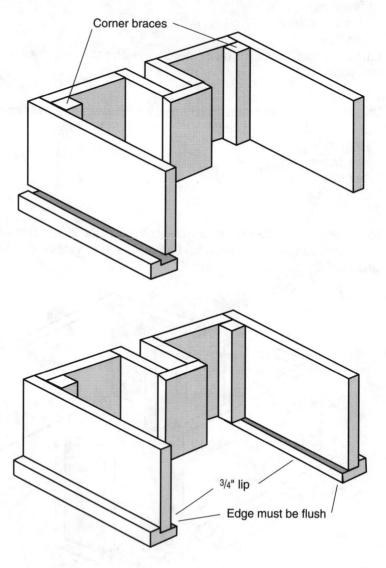

Corner braces

3/4" lip

Edge must be flush

Measure and cut the pieces that will form the shelf and the shelf supports. Attach the shelf supports to the shelf using glue and screws. Next—again using glue and screws—attach the shelf assembly to the inside of the router bench. Clamp this assembly into position and allow it to dry.

Step 4

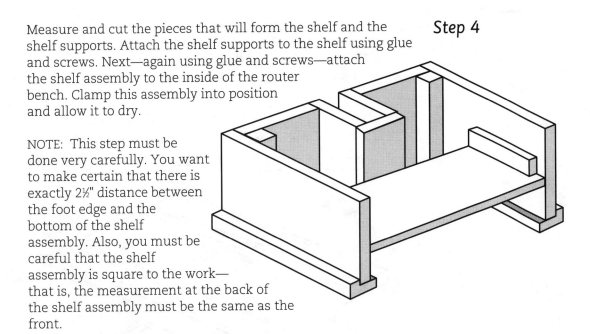

NOTE: This step must be done very carefully. You want to make certain that there is exactly 2½" distance between the foot edge and the bottom of the shelf assembly. Also, you must be careful that the shelf assembly is square to the work— that is, the measurement at the back of the shelf assembly must be the same as the front.

Measure and cut the router bench table or top. As shown in the illustration, cut an opening 8¼" square in the center, and cut a 1¾"-x-1½" notch in the center back.

Step 5

Measure and cut the walnut trim strips for the top and the front of the router bench. Then glue and nail the strips in place using a countersink. Fill the holes with wood filler.

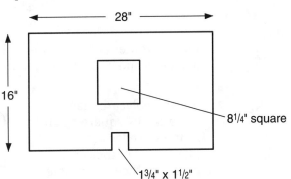

28"

16"

8¼" square

1³/4" x 1¹/2"

Attach the router table to the router bench frame, centering it with the back flush to the frame. Attach it to the frame using countersunk screws and glue.

Step 6

Using a router with a dovetail bit, rout two ⅜"-deep grooves, as shown. I elected to make the back groove 1" wide and the front groove 1½" wide so that I could have a wider base for the miter gauge I would use in the front of the router.

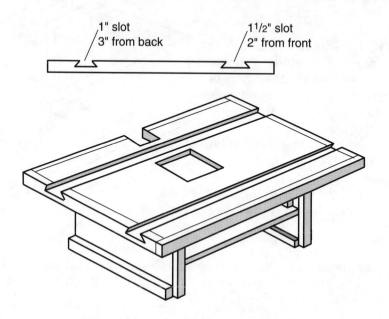

1" slot
3" from back

1½" slot
2" from front

Using a router and a ½" straight bit with a bottom bearing, rout a ¼" deep and wide rabbet around the center cutout.

Step 7   Cut the polycarbonate material 8½" square. Slightly round the edges so that the plate fits into the center cutout of the router table.

Remove the base plate from your router and center in on the polycarbonate sheet. Mark the locations for the screw holes and the center hole (the router bit opening). This step is crucial because

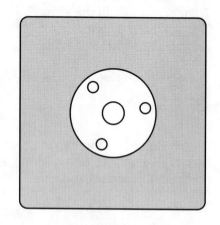

the router bit must sit exactly in the center of this hole for you to use any sort of adapter, such as a template guide.

Drill the center hole and the holes for the countersunk base plate screws. Take care to countersink the base plate screws just enough for them to clear the surface, but not enough for them to catch on any work surface.

The polycarbonate will melt or curl around the cutout area. Take a small pocket knife to clean up this residual material.

Step 8

Attach the polycarbonate to the bottom of the router, and store your baseplate for later use. Put this assembly into the router table and adjust all corners so that the fit is snug and absolutely flush with the table surface.

Wiring (optional)

I wired the router bench so that it had a switch and outlet for the router as shown in the photo. Do not attempt this step, however, unless you have a knowledge of electrical wiring.

Step 9

Measure and cut the wood pieces that will form the drawer assembly. The sides are 2¼" × 9½", the back is 2¼" × 20¾", and the front piece is 2¼" × 22⅜". The bottom is cut from plywood and is 9½" × 22⅜". Assemble these pieces using screws and glue.

The ultimate router bench 65

Measure and cut the drawer facing 3½" × 24". I used red oak and routed a cove edge on the front. Center and attach the facing to the drawer assembly using screws and glue.

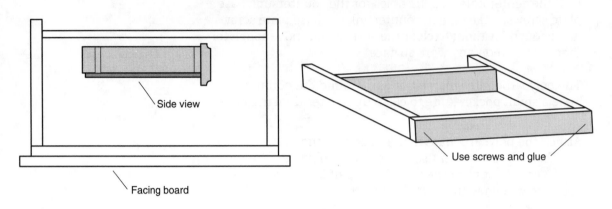

Side view

Facing board

Use screws and glue

Step 10   Measure and cut the pieces forming the router fence assembly. (See the materials list for the sizes of all of the pieces.) Next, assemble all of the pieces forming the fence base or back (as shown), using screws and glue.

The back should be aligned to put pressure on the mini fence when the fence is clamped to the router table.

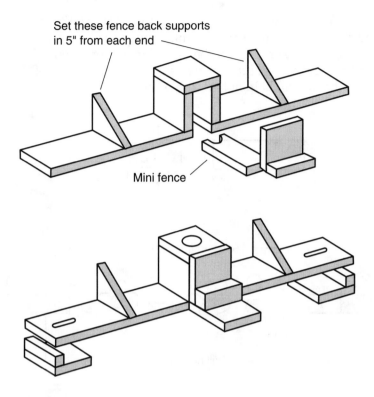

Set these fence back supports in 5" from each end

Mini fence

The fence clamping mechanism is nothing more than a 3"-×-5½" length of wood with a 1" rocker strip. It is held in place and clamped to the router table surface with a 3" carriage bolt and a wing nut or with a special knob, such as the one shown. This knob—which has a mating nut imbedded in it and is held in place with epoxy—will make tightening the carriage bolt much easier.

Step 11

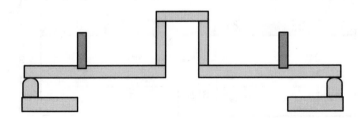

Step 12   Center and drill a ⅜" hole into the bottom rocker strip board and the ends of the fence. You might want to allow a 1" hole ⅜" wide so the rocker strip can be moved in for some fence-lock positions. Adding a small strip of sandpaper to the top of the rocker board will help hold it into position better.

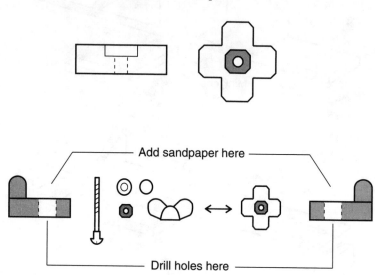

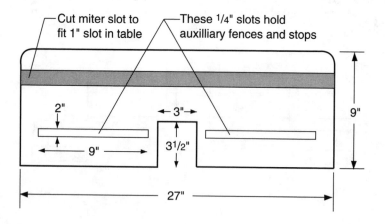

Step 13   The fence face is cut from laminate-coated particleboard, but you can substitute plywood. Center and attach the fence face to the rear fence with glue and countersunk screws. Finally, drill a hole in the top of the rear fence to fit the hose extension of your shop vacuum.

68 Workshop accessories you can make

Measure and cut the polycarbonate to fit the rear router. Make an arc of a circle at one end as shown. Drop in about a half inch, and cut a slot a little over ¼" wide. Drill starter holes at both ends and cut with a saber saw set at a very slow speed. (You can also do this with a router mounted on a circle cutting jig. However, the high speed of the router could cause the polycarbonate to melt, in which case you will have to clean up the edges with a pocket knife.)

Step 14

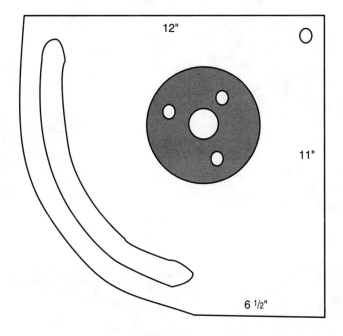

Remove the router plate from the router you intend to use on the polycarbonate, and center and outline the openings for the router bit and the screws to hold the router in place. Drill the holes for the router bit opening and countersink the holes for the screws to hold the router in place.

Step 15

Mount the polycarbonate router plate to the back of the router bench or table, and center the opening for the router bit in the back slot or opening. I used a 1½" drywall screw with a washer at the pivot point to hold the plate in place. At the slot area, I recommend that you use a threaded insert for a ¼" machine screw and a matching washer and wing nut. Make certain that

The ultimate router bench 69

once positioned, the router is securely locked into position before using it. Then mount the router to the polycarbonate and position it for a test cut.

70 Workshop accessories you can make

The next step is to make the miter gauges. Measure and cut two ⅜"-thick pieces of hardwood 11" long for the miter gauge to sit on and to fit into the 1" and 1½" slots in the router table surface. This is best done using the router table and a dovetail bit to cut the appropriate angle. You want these pieces to fit into the slots snugly, but with freedom to move.

Step 16

Measure and cut the two miter gauges from hardwood. Cut a ¼" slot in the rounded end as shown. Drill a centered, countersunk hole in the front, flat end of the gauges, as shown in the drawing.

Step 17

Attach the miter gauges to the sliding base using a drywall screw in the front centered hole and a flat-headed stove bolt mounted from underneath the sliding base, recessed or countersunk. Attach a mating washer and wing nut to hold the miter gauge into the proper position.

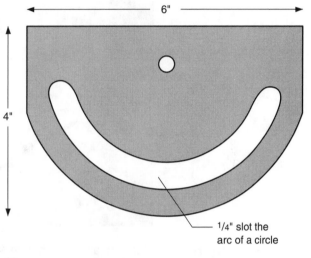

6"

4"

1/4" slot the arc of a circle

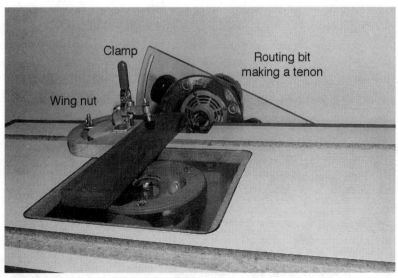

Clamp

Routing bit making a tenon

Wing nut

The ultimate router bench 71

Optional clamping mechanism

An optional step is to add a clamping mechanism, such as the one shown, to hold the work in place. These can be purchased at most woodworking stores or through woodworking magazines and catalogs. If you are really clever, you can make your own.

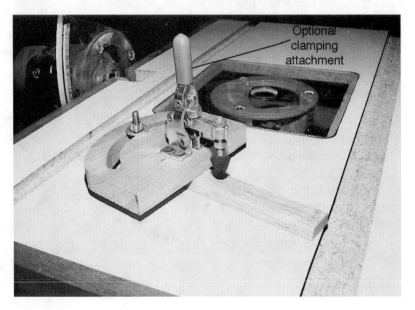

Optional clamping attachment

Step 18

Measure and cut the pieces forming the fence stops, which are 3" × 3½". These stops are mounted to the fence using 2 flat-headed stove bolts, ⅛" × 2", with matching washers and wing nuts.

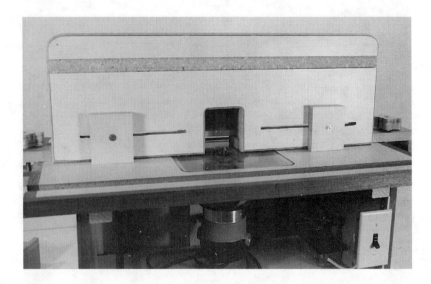

You can add any number of auxiliary fences and other attachments to the base fence—such as a circular-work shaping or routing fence or a flat-circle cutting fence or jig.

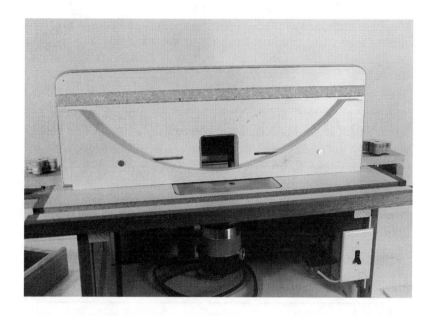

Sliding fence

Step 1 The sliding fence for making dovetails and box joints is simple to make. Measure and cut two sliding dovetails, as described in in step 17. These will be the base for the sliding fence.

Step 2 Measure and cut the pieces forming the box-joint-and-dovetail sliding fence. Cut the face from laminate-covered particleboard, the adjustable face from ½" Baltic birch plywood, the supports from 1" pine, and the window from polycarbonate.

Step 3 The crucial part of this assembly is squaring the face of the fence with the sliding bases and the router tabletop. The best way to do this is to slide the bases into the miter-gauge slots in the router tabletop. Next, center the fence face on top of these bases. Using a square, position the face square to the tabletop and the sliding bases. Glue and screw the support blocks to the fence and then to the sliding bases. Allow this setup to dry before proceeding.

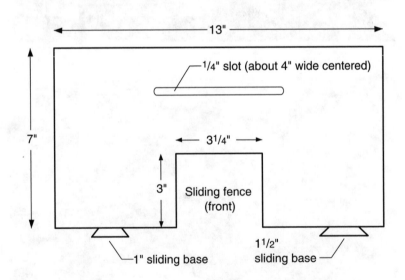

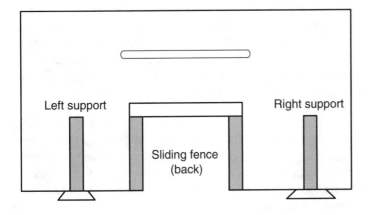

Left support   Right support

Sliding fence
(back)

Remove the assembly from the router tabletop, and add one more screw through the bottom of the sliding base, countersinking the screw into the bottom of the face. Put the assembly back into the router tabletop, and recheck the square.

Attach the back of the fence including the polycarbonate window using glue and screws.

Step 4

Step 5   The adjustable face is designed to move left or right of the router cutter. Attach it to the face using a ¼" flat-headed stove bolt that has been countersunk and is aligned with the slot cut into the face. Position the board and tighten the adjustable fence to the face with a wing nut and washer. You will need one of these for box joints and one for dovetail joints.

Cut a slot in the adjustable fence and glue in place a small wood block the size of the block joint or dovetail you intend to cut, positioning it slightly off-center. This will allow you to move the adjustable fence to the left or right of the cutter to make the box joint or dovetail with the appropriate distance between the joints.

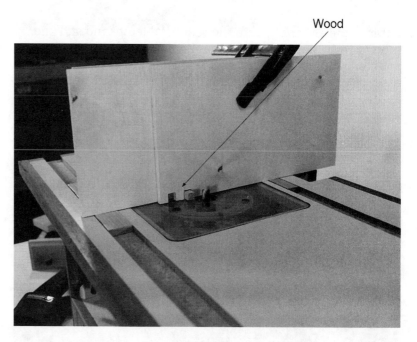

Wood

Step 6   Position the work, clamp it to the adjustable fence, and make the first cut. Then slip that cut over the small wood block, and cut the next.

Pin router attachment

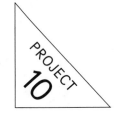

THE PIN ROUTER ATTACHMENT shown here is easy to make and extends the use of your router table by allowing you to make intricate cuts in wood by following a pattern. With it, you can make cutting boards with grooves, cheese trays, and inlays for all kinds of projects. The pin can be made in various sizes to allow you to follow both patterns that are very narrow and those ones that are wider. You can move the pin up and down by adjusting the wing nut and bolt holding it in place. In addition, you can adjust the whole assembly by adjusting the bolt and wing nut that hold the assembly to the router table in the back.

Materials	½" Baltic birch plywood 1 square foot 2 pieces pin board support 2¾" × 7" 1 piece V wedge frame 7" × 8" 1 piece 8" × 4" back support 1" hardwood 2½" × 12" pin support 2 × 4 1½" × 2¼" × 11" slot guide
Hardware & miscellaneous	Carpenter's wood glue 6 drywall screws 1" 1 stove bolt ¼" × 3" with wing nut and washer 1 piece ¾" wood dowel 10" 1 piece ¼" wood dowel 2" 1 piece ½" wood dowel 2"
Tools required	Drill with ¼", ¾" bits and countersink Screwdriver Saber saw Circular saw
Step 1	Measure and cut the Baltic birch as shown in the diagram. The two wedge cutoffs will be used to support the router pin support. Trim 1" off of the wide end of each wedge.

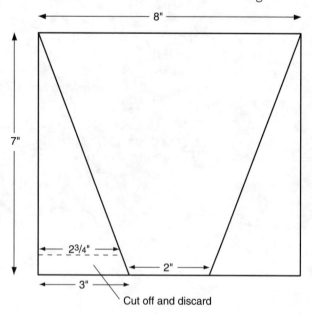

Measure and cut the hardwood router pin support board as shown. Round or taper the front end of the board. Drill a ¾" hole centered in the front of the board as shown. Then cut a ⅜" slot in the front, as shown, and drill a ¼" hole in the side for a stove bolt to be inserted. Glue the wedge cutoffs onto the main center wedge as shown.

Step 2

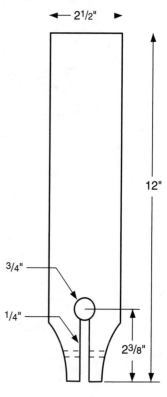

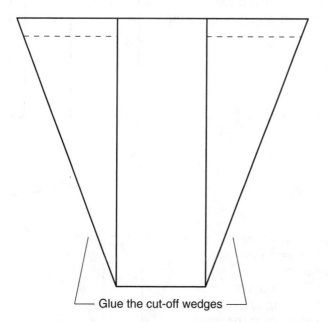

Glue the cut-off wedges

Measure and cut the back support board from the Baltic birch, and attach it to the main center wedge as the dotted lines indicate.

Step 3

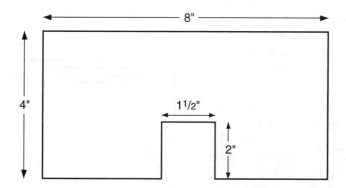

Pin router attachment 79

Step 4 Measure and cut to size the 2×4 piece that forms the basic spine of the unit, the slot guide. Two inches from the top of the board, cut a slot in the center of this guide, ½" wide and about 3" long. Attach this to the other assembly using screws and glue centered.

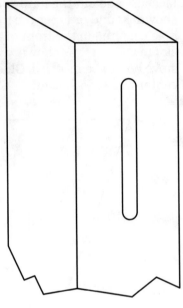

Step 5 Glue the router pin support board into the center of the assembly. Test it first to make certain that it is going to put the pin dead-center over the router bit. I suggest that you put a small veining bit in the router chuck for this test. Because this step is so crucial to the usefulness of your router pin attachment, you must take the time to do it right, or pay the price later.

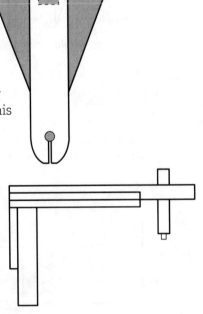

The router pin is made by drilling a ¼" and/or a ½" hole into the center of the ¾" dowel rod. Cut off 4" pieces of this rod and center the drill very carefully when

80 Workshop accessories you can make

performing this task. I suggest that you use hardwood dowels for this purpose. Cut off only about an inch of the smaller dowels, and expose them only by about ⅜". If you have them, metal pins this size or nylon guides would be preferable to the wood dowel rods. In any event, make certain that the pins are glued in securely.

Tenoning jig

A TENONING JIG CAN turn your router table into a true tenoning device. If you use it with a half-inch or larger veining bit, you can make rungs for chairs all day long. The only limitations are the length of the bit, which is usually about ¾" long—more than adequate for most tenons. Its construction is quite simple. All you need is a 2 × 4 fence and a special mold or form for holding the square or round stock while you turn it to form the tenon.

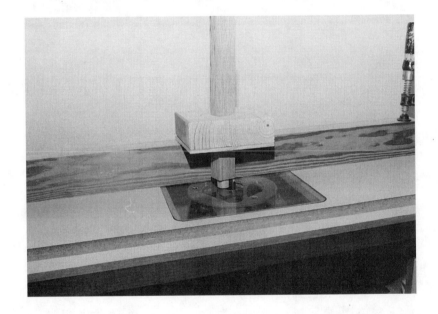

Materials
2 × 4 stock 36"
  1 piece 30" long for fence
  1 piece 3" diameter
    round to hold tenon
2 × 6 stock 5" × 5" square
  for mold or form

Hardware & miscellaneous
3 drywall screws 2½"
6 finishing nails 1"
1 piece ¼" plywood 5" × 5"
2 C-clamps

Tools required
Saber saw or band saw
Drill with ½" bit
Screwdriver

Measure and cut the 2 × 4 fence to size, then measure and cut a **Step 1**
3"-diameter block or circle from the 2 × 4 stock. Finally,
measure and cut a 5"-square block
from 2 × 6 wood stock.

Using the round block or circle of
wood as a template, draw a similar
circle in the center of the 5"-square
block of 2 × 6. Drill a starter hole
with a drill and bit, and cut out the
excess with a saber saw.

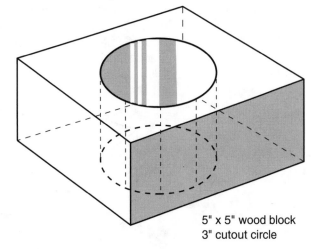

5" x 5" wood block
3" cutout circle

Slip the 3" circle of wood into the 5"-square block, checking to **Step 2**
ensure it rotates smoothly. If it does not, repeat the process. It
is very important that this circle of wood turns smoothly.

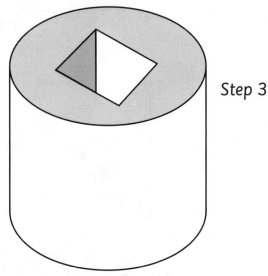

Next, cut an opening for the
tenon size you are using in the
circle of wood. The opening
can be either square or round;
in fact, you might want to
keep several different sizes of
openings for different widths
of tenons.

Step 3

Step 4   Measure and cut a piece of ¼" plywood to fit on the base of the block, as shown. Measure and cut a circle into the center of the plywood that is smaller than the circle or round block by at least ½". Attach the plywood to the bottom of the 5" block using finishing nails and glue. Insert the round wood block and again check that it revolves smoothly.

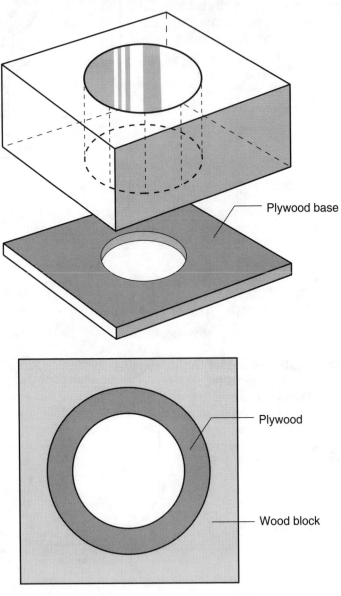

Plywood base

Plywood

Wood block

84 Workshop accessories you can make

Attach the subassembly you made in step 4 to the center of the **Step 5**
2 × 4 wood fence using screws and glue. Clamp the assembly
over the router bit and begin your tenon-
making operation.

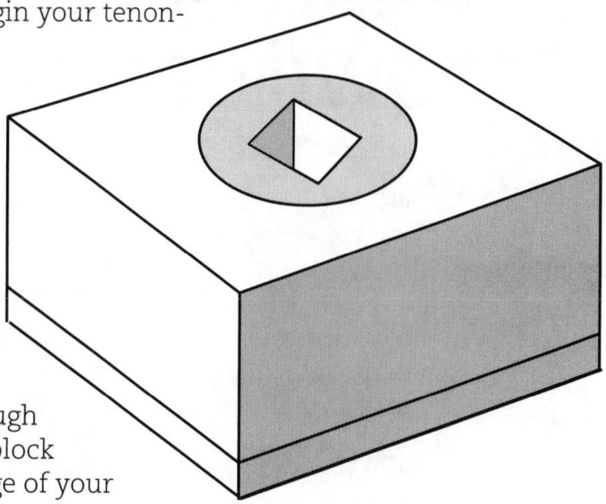

NOTE: The tenon must
rest on top of the
polycarbonate router
plate. It must have this
surface to ride on to
ensure a proper cut.

To begin operations,
turn on the router and
slowly ease the work through
the opening in the round block
downward, so that the edge of your
wood form feeds into the blade. Rotate the
work slowly to form the tenon.

Inverted saber saw/jigsaw

With a polycarbonate sheet attached to its bottom, your saber saw can become a jigsaw. Simply mount the configuration into a recessed cutout in your work bench or router table. This frees your hands for feeding work into the blade while providing better control over the work. By using a polycarbonate strip for a hold-down, you can do all sorts of intricate and fine-detail work that is not possible with a handheld saber saw. I attached this assembly to my ultimate router table (see project 9) so that I could use the on/off switch and standardize on the size of the polycarbonate sheet.

Materials

2 × 4 10" long, hold down support
Polycarbonate material 1 square foot ¼" thick
  1 piece 8½" long base plate
  1 piece 1½" × 12" hold-down

1 carriage bolt ⅜" × 4" with washer and wing nut
3 flat headed stove bolts ¼" × 1" with washer and nut
3 drywall screws 1½"

Drill with countersink and ⅜" bit
Saber saw
Screwdriver

Tools required

Measure and cut the 2×4 stock 12" × 1½" × 2". This will form the
hold-down support. Cut one end at a slight angle. Drill two ⅜"
holes at each end of the hold-down support, and cut out the
excess using a saber saw.

Step 1

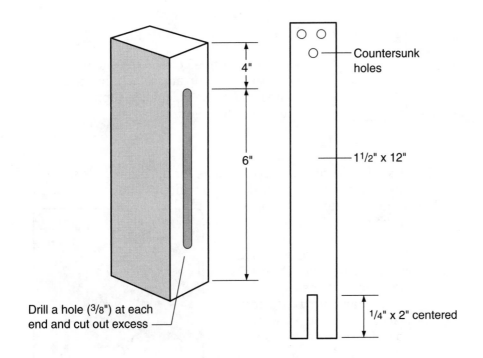

4"

6"

Drill a hole (3/8") at each
end and cut out excess

Countersunk
holes

1¹/2" x 12"

1/4" x 2" centered

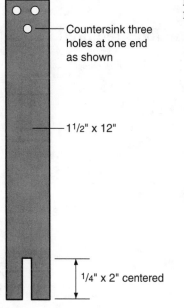

Countersink three
holes at one end
as shown

1¹/2" x 12"

¹/4" x 2" centered

Step 2 Measure and cut the polycarbonate strip as shown, and sand the edges slightly to remove any sharpness. Heat the tip of the polycarbonate strip and bend it so that the bent edge will fit right over the tip of the saber-saw blade.

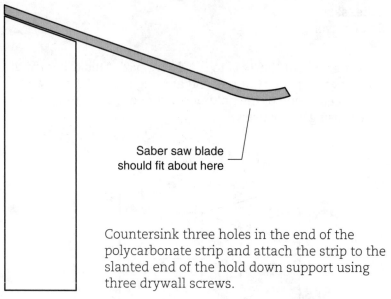

Saber saw blade
should fit about here

Countersink three holes in the end of the polycarbonate strip and attach the strip to the slanted end of the hold down support using three drywall screws.

Step 3 Measure and cut the polycarbonate for the base of the saber saw. Remember that it is designed to fit into the opening of the ultimate router bench (project 9), which is 8½" square.

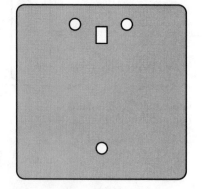

The drawing for the base plate is only a suggestion. You must place your saber saw on top of the base and draw the actual places where you must cut holes for the blade to go through, and also where you wish to drill holes.

I suggest that you first drill three ¼" countersunk holes into your saber saw base plate, and then mark the positions on the

88 Workshop accessories you can make

polycarbonate. Then remove the base plate or shoe of the saber saw to drill the holes into the metal shoe. I opted to drill two holes in the front and one in the back. Remember to do this operation very carefully, as you want the blade of the saw to be square to the polycarbonate plate when you are done.

Attach the base plate to the saber saw using the 1" stove bolts with washers, lock washers, and nuts. Insert this assembly into the router table insert area. (I opted to use the on/off switch on the router table, but that step is optional.)

Step 4

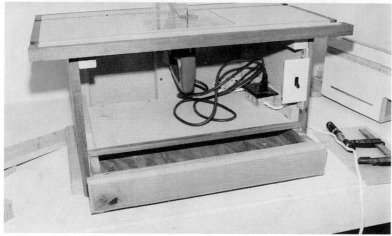

Inverted saber saw/jigsaw 89

Step 5   Attach the hold down assembly to the slot in the router table as shown. Use a carriage bolt with a wing nut and a lock washer to hold the assembly properly in place.

To use this setup properly, adjust the hold-down so that enough pressure is on the work so that it will not bounce up and down when fed into the saw blade. This takes practice, and I suggest you take the time to try out this project using some scrap wood. Also, when cutting wood thicker than 1", be very careful about the feed rate; if you feed the saw wood too fast, the blade will tend to bend, giving less-than-desirable results.

Bench vice

YOU CAN LITERALLY SPEND hundreds of dollars for a bench vice. Some models on the market go for over $400. In fact, a bench-vice screw alone, minus the guts of the vice, can sometimes cost over $100. You can part with that kind of money, or you can go down to your local home center, buy a few odds and ends, and make your own bench vice. And guess what? You can make a darn good one for less than a tenth of the cost of those fancy, store-bought kind.

The components that make up this bench vice are off-the-shelf items you can buy at any home center. The threaded steel shafts that you can buy at these home centers have about twice the threads per linear inch than that of a normal bench screw, which means that the bench vice you are about to make will be slow to open and close. For this reason, if you are prone to fits of impatience, have anxiety attacks, and drink too much coffee, this project is definitely not for you. If, on the other

hand, you are not easily riled, are not in a hurry, and want to save a lot of money, this is a project you will really appreciate!

I specified a threaded rod 36" long because that is the most common length available. If you have a hacksaw, I recommend that you reduce that length to about 24", thereby reducing the weight hanging out under the end of your workbench and making it easier to open and close. Of course, if you want to be able to have that kind of length in your bench vice, you can stick with the 36".

Materials

1 x 12 hardwood lumber 4 linear feet
   3 pieces 8" × 10" vice jaws
   2 pieces 5" × 10" support pieces
   7 pieces 3½" diameter handle shaft assembly
   8 pieces 2½" diameter handle ends
   4 pieces 2" diameter bench dogs
   4 pieces 1" V wedges for dowels
½" Baltic birch 1 square foot
   1 piece 8" × 10" vice jaw center

Hardware & miscellaneous

3 pieces hardwood wood dowel 1" × 36"
1 piece polycarbonate ⅜" thick 4" diameter
1 threaded steel shaft ¾" to 1" × 36"
5 matching nuts with 3 lock washers
Epoxy
Carpenter's glue
WD-40 or Vaseline
Beeswax
2 pieces ¼" × 1" × 2" aluminum strip
16 drywall screws 1¼"

Tools required

Wood clamps
Drill with ¾", 1" & 1¼" spade bits and countersink
Saber saw or band saw
Screwdriver
Router with a rounding over bit

Measure and cut the five vice-jaw components from hardwood: **Step 1**
3 pieces 8" × 10" (call these pieces components A) and 2 pieces
5" × 10" (call these pieces components B). Measure and cut the vice-jaw component from the ½" Baltic birch or some equivalent plywood.

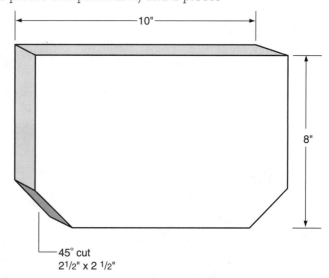

10"

8"

45° cut
2¹/₂" x 2 ¹/₂"

Stack all of the components from step 1 together in one big **Step 2**
sandwich. Make certain that they are all even, then clamp
them to hold them aligned. Next, drill three 1" holes as shown.
Make certain that the holes are drilled absolutely straight. In
fact, this is an operation where a drill press is preferred but not
absolutely necessary if you are careful.

Bench vice 93

Cut a 4¼" hole into the center of the Baltic birch plywood. This will house the polycarbonate piece later when the bench vice is laminated to form the jaws. Make absolutely certain that this is dead center to the 1" hole.

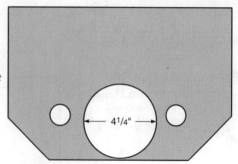

Step 3 Measure and cut the ⅜" polycarbonate (Lexan) into a 4" circle. Sand the edges slightly to remove any sharp edges. In the absolute center of the 4" circle, drill a hole the same diameter as the threaded rod you are using.

Remove the protective backing and facing, and attach the polycarbonate to the threaded rod as shown. Place the polycarbonate between nuts and lock washers about 5" from one end of the rod. Tighten the nuts as tight as you can get them.

Step 4

Next drill a hole in the center of two of the A vice jaw pieces, or enlarge the 1" hole already there. You need a hole big enough to allow these pieces to slip over the nut and lock washer. I used a ¾" threaded rod and matching lock washers and nuts; therefore I drilled a 1¼" hole. The important thing is that the nuts should be able to turn freely when centered in the hole.

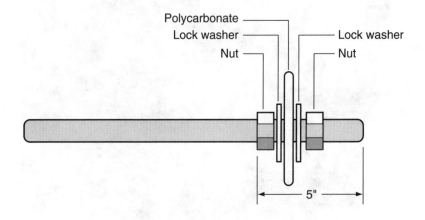

Polycarbonate

Lock washer — — Lock washer

Nut — — Nut

5"

Bench vice 95

Step 5   Make a sandwich out of the plywood and the two A pieces from step 4, placing them around the polycarbonate on the rod. I suggest that you align the pieces by placing two 1" wooden dowels through the right and left holes in each of these pieces. Glue them and clamp them securely, and let this assembly dry thoroughly before proceeding. Meanwhile, make certain that the rod turns freely in the assembly.

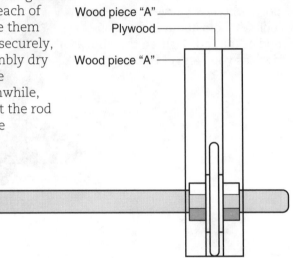

Wood piece "A"

Plywood

Wood piece "A"

Next take one of the pieces marked B and enlarge the 1" holes in the left and right sides by about ¼". Position one of the nuts over the center 1" hole, and mark the outline of the nut onto the board. Using a chisel, cut the nut form into the wood to a depth of about ¼".

Using epoxy, glue the nut into this hole. Take great care not to get any of the epoxy into the nut threads. Allow this assembly to set up, and then go on to the next step.

Step 6

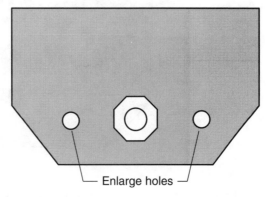

Enlarge holes

Shim the epoxied washer with two aluminum strips and screws. Drill two holes in the edge of a large washer and place it over the nut. Hold this in place with two 1¼" drywall screws. Make certain there is room for the threaded shaft to go through the washer hole. Attach this assembly to the lower back of one of the vice jaws using screws and glue.

Step 7

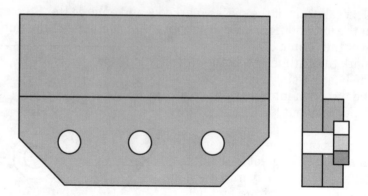

Step 8 Measure and cut the circles that will form the handle assembly. Drill one in the center the size necessary to slip over the front of the threaded rod. Round the edges with a router and a rounding-over bit, and place it over the threaded rod as shown. Using a square, verify that the shaft is square to the front vice jaw. (I did this by clamping the assembly to the edge of a work bench and letting the rod hang down.) Once you have the rod squared to the vice jaw, glue and screw the rounded piece into place. Recess the screws and cover the holes with wood plugs. Sand smooth.

98 Workshop accessories you can make

Attach the threaded rod to the assembly from step 7. Also attach the 1" dowels. Most wooden dowels are slightly smaller than the rated dimension, so the 1" dowels should slip into the 1" holes fairly easily. If not, you will have to sand the holes slightly so that they do fit.

Cut ½" saw kerfs in the end of each dowel. Glue them into the front and rear jaw vice assemblies. Tap small wood wedges into the saw kerfs, tightening the wooden dowels in the ends. Allow this assembly to dry before proceeding.

Step 9

Next, cut off the excess wood wedges and sand the face jaws so the surface is flush. Add some WD40 or some similar lubricant to the threaded rod and to the nut. Also rub beeswax on the wooden dowels so that they slide easily in the holes of the rear vice jaw assembly.

Step 10

Center a nut on two of the handle-shaft assembly pieces and mark the outline of the nut. Using a chisel or a saber saw—and with a pilot hole drilled so that the blade can get through—cut out an opening so that the nut will fit inside of this round piece of wood.

Step 11   Start the handle assembly by putting a nut onto the rod. You will have to experiment here. You want the nut to be about 1" from the front of the face of the vice. Using a hammer and a metal chisel, damage the threads on the rod.

Next, screw the nut into these damaged threads until it gets stuck. Place one of the nut-cutout round pieces over that nut, and epoxy it in place. While the epoxy is drying, drill a hole in the center of one other round piece the size of the shaft. Place that over the rod and screw it to the first one with two recessed drywall screws.

Add a lock washer and a nut and tighten this first assembly as tight as you can make it. Place the next circle with the nut cutout over the last nut, and epoxy it in place. Add two recessed drywall screws, also.

Now add each of the remaining round wood pieces using screws and glue. Keep the screws to the outside of the round wooden pieces because later you are going to drill a 1" hole through the center of this shaft and you need to avoid hitting those screws. NOTE: I routed the first and the last round piece

100 Workshop accessories you can make

with a router and a rounding-over bit to soften the appearances. I also did the same to the face of the front vice jaw assembly.

Drill a 1" hole in the handle assembly as shown. (Remember to remember where you put the screws.) Sand the final assembly to remove any rough edges and to compensate for any of the rounded pieces that might have been slightly off. Cut one of the 1" wood dowels to a length of about 24".

Step 12

Step 13

Measure and cut the eight round wood pieces that will make up the handle ends. Stack the round pieces 4 up, and glue and clamp them. After the glue has dried, drill a 1" hole, centered, into the ends of this assembly to a depth of about 2".

Insert the wood dowel into the handle assembly and add the end pieces by gluing them in place. I also drilled two holes into the top of the front vice jaw assembly so that I could add the use of bench dogs later.

The ultimate workbench

THIS WORKBENCH EVOLVED over the years in my own workshop. I wanted something with a big work surface that could have multiple applications—something that could hold one project at one end and yet allow the construction of another at the other end. It has plenty of bench dog holes for many uses. It has two vices: One the standard record-type and one an end vice. The end has a tool crib or box for storing things out of the way and usually winds up with a lot of my junk stuff that has to be cleaned out periodically.

This bench is big, and it is not cheap to make. It has a large 4 × 4 frame that supports the top. The top has a center core of 25 2 × 4s "laminated" together. The box or tool crib is attached to the center core at one end and the whole thing is then wrapped with 1" hardwoods. The record vice is integrated into the wrap, and the inner jaw facing is part of the wrap boards.

The end vice is integrated into the bench design, and laminations of hardwood out from the center core complete the design.

I drilled 1" holes in the surface to hold bench dogs and cam dog clamps of my own design (see project 1). Similar holes are in the end and side vice faces for the use of bench dogs and for holding projects in place. There are a few additional things that I am going to add to this bench, but for now it is pretty sophisticated as it is.

Materials

4 × 4 pine, fir or hardwood 48 linear feet
    4 pieces 64" center dividers
    4 pieces 32" end dividers
    4 pieces 34" posts
2 × 4 pine, fir or hardwood 150 linear feet
    25 pieces 2" × 72" center core
1 × 4 red oak 32 linear feet
    2 pieces 3½" × 38" core ends
    1 piece 2" × 7½" back
    1 piece 2" × 40½" back
    4 pieces 2" × 57" back
1 × 6 red oak 19 linear feet
    2 pieces 5½" × 7¾" box ends
    2 pieces 5½" × 42½" box sides
    1 piece 5½" × 38¾" side wrap
    3 pieces 5½" × 12" end vice face
    2 pieces 16" end vice sides
    1 piece 12" record vice face
    2 pieces 2" × 15⅛" end vice box
    2 pieces 3₁₆" × 2¾" end vice box
    1 piece 3¾" × 16¼" end vice top
    3 pieces 12" end vice end
    1 piece 73½" inner back wrap
1 × 6 walnut 21 linear feet
    1 piece 84½" front facing
    1 piece 67" back facing
    1 piece 42½" end wrap
    1 piece 18½" end vice side
    1 piece 13½" end vice face
    1 piece 2¼" end vice side

1 piece 13½" record vice face
4 pieces ¾" × ¾" × 33¼" Top and bottom side trim
4 pieces ¾" × ¾" × 21" side end trim
2 pieces ¾" × ¾" × 21" front end trim
2 pieces ¾" × ¾" × 57" front top and bottom trim
¼" red oak plywood 4 × 8 sheet
2 pieces 21" × 33¼" sides
1 piece 21" × 57" front insert
1 piece 7" × 41¾" box bottom

Hardware & miscellaneous

32 wood screws 5"
Handful wood screws 1½"
Handful wood screws 2½d"
1 record vice model 52½D
End vice hardware
Carpenter's glue
Danish oil
80 or so 1" finishing nails
4 lag screws ⁵⁄₁₆" × 2½" and washers
Handful wood plugs

Tools required

Drill with countersink and ¼" & 1" bits
Screwdriver
Circular saw
Router with rounding-over, cove, and straight bits
Belt sander

2×4 workbench materials

2 × 4 fir or pine 190 linear feet
22 pieces part A top slat 6
1 piece part B backstop 6
2 pieces part C outer slat 65"
2 pieces part D side brace 65"
4 pieces part E legs 35"
4 pieces part F end brace 33"
3 pieces part G braces 7"
¾" plywood 36" x 72" shelf

Hardware & miscellaneous

140 wood screws 2"
Carpenter's glue

104 Workshop accessories you can make

Drill with countersink
Circular saw
Screwdriver

Start by building the base frame. Measure and cut all of the base components as listed in the materials list. Next, notch the posts and the center dividers as shown. I suggest that you cut the basic notches with a handheld circular saw by making repeat cuts and then knocking out the scrap with a chisel. While there are many basic joints that I could select for this assembly, I think this one is the easiest for most people to follow.

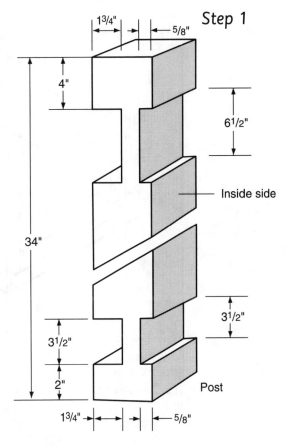

Step 1

1³/4"
5/8"
4"
6¹/2"
Inside side
34"
3¹/2"
3¹/2"
2"
Post
1³/4"
5/8"

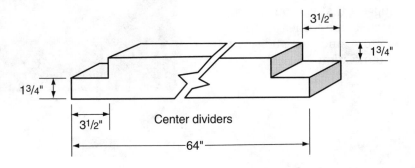

3¹/2"
1³/4"
1³/4"
3¹/2"
Center dividers
64"

The ultimate workbench 105

Step 2   Assemble the components and do a dry-
run assembly. Put all of the pieces
together and hold in them place
with clamps while you survey
the assembly for mistakes
and make corrections as
necessary.

The final assembly is with screws and glue. Put four 5" wood
screws into each joint and recess them, covering the screw

head with a wood plug. I strongly
suggest that you let this assembly
set overnight before moving on to
the next step. Although they are
not shown in these illustrations, I
suggest that you put V-wedges at
each inside corner at the top and
bottom, and glue and screw them
into position.

I put side and front panels in the base assembly. They are very easy to make and require only plywood-panel inserts and trim or molding to go around the inside of the basic frame. I used red oak plywood and walnut trim that I ripped to ¾" square and then routed with a cove bit to hold them in place.

I suggest that you glue and nail the walnut trim into place about 2" from the front lip of the 4 × 4 frame front and sides. Then slip the panels in from the inside, holding them in place with glue and small finishing nails.

The next step is to cut 25 2 × 4s to length (72"), and rip them to 2" strips. These will form the center core of the workbench top.

Step 4

2 x 4 Workbench core

Step 5   This step is crucial. You are going to use glue and the 2½"
screws to attach the 1½"-wide-x-2"-deep strips to form the
center core. You must perfectly align the top so that the boards
are flush. If you do not, you will use bad words at the end of
this project because a sanding job will be in order to straighten
up your goof. A second point of importance is that you must
use screws and remember where you put them so that when
you drill the bench top holes you will not hit a screw. (And
don't blame me if you ruin a drill bit!)

A tip: Glue and clamp the boards securely before you use the
screws. Also, countersink the screws so the next boards can fit
flush.

Another good point: Do this on a flat surface, such as the
garage floor, so that the assembly is flat and not warped, and
be sure to use good, straight lumber. I used some pressure-
treated lumber, Wolmanized Extra, that was leftover from a
deck job, but any good, straight lumber will do. If you elect to
use a hardwood, make certain you have lots of friendly
neighbors since you will need them to lift this thing in place.

If you do not take the time to do this step right, the final part of
the assembly will be your worst nightmare.

Step 6   I am making the assumption that you
goofed in step 5. Sanding is one way to
correct the problem. You can also
smooth the surface by using a router
with a straight bit supported on
guide boards. This will take out
the really rough spots, but
you'll still need to use
a sander for the
final step.

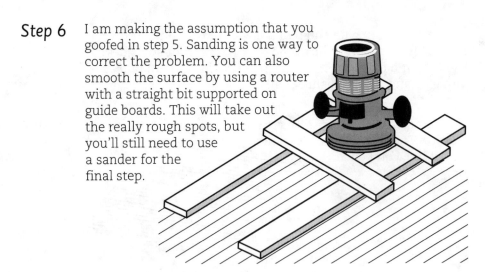

Measure and cut the oak strips that go on the ends of the core assembly. Attach them with screws and glue so that they are flush with the top and sides.

Step 7

The next step is to make the tool crib or box that goes at the end of the core assembly. So that we get our lingo right, I am referring to the front part of the bench where we have the *Weekend Workshop* logo (see the project photo, page 102). The back part is where the vices are, and the left side is where the box or tool crib goes.

Step 8

Measure and cut the four pieces of oak that will form the sides of the box. Also cut the plywood sheet forming the bottom of the box. Using a circular saw or a router with a straight bit, rout a ¼"-wide-x-⅜"-deep dado ¼" from the bottom of all four boards.

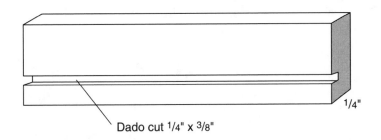

1/4"

Dado cut ¼" x ⅜"

Assemble all four boards with the plywood bottom in place, and then glue and screw, recessing the screws in the sides. Do not glue in the plywood panel.

Step 9

Attach the box or crib to the left side of the core assembly using screws and glue. Recess the screws and fill the holes with wood plugs. Make certain that the crib is flush with the front and the top of the core assembly.

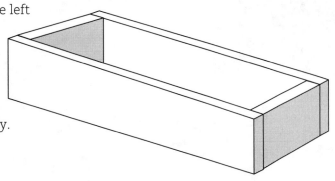

The ultimate workbench 109

Step 10 Next, start the build-up of the back part of the bench top by using first a 5½-x-73½" strip and four 2-x-57-inch pieces of red oak. The first board must be cut so that 24" is a full 5½". The remainder is cut to only 2" of width. This is so you have adequate facing for the attachment of the end vice and yet narrow enough at the other end so the record vice will fit.

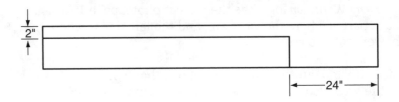

Cut the first board and attach it using screws and glue. Attach the remaining four boards to the left as shown. Remember to countersink the screws and keep the boards flush with the top of the bench top.

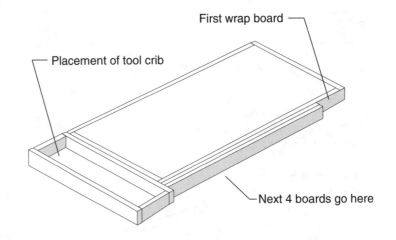

First wrap board

Placement of tool crib

Next 4 boards go here

The next step is to attach the record vice hardware. Attach a 7½-x-2" strip of red oak to the right of the tool crib. Next attach the record vice so that it butts up against the board you just installed. The vice jaw is exactly ¾" thick, so it should be flush to the left with the board you just installed.

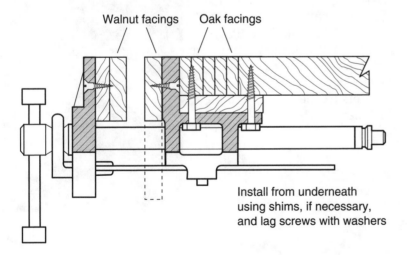

Walnut facings   Oak facings

Install from underneath
using shims, if necessary,
and lag screws with washers

Attach the back board to the right of the vice using screws and glue. It is 2" × 40½". Measure and cut the walnut strip that goes across the vice on the inside, as shown in the photo. Attach this using screws and glue. While you're at it, go ahead and attach the walnut strip in the front of the bench and on the left by the tool crib. Countersink the screws and fill the holes with walnut wood plugs.

Measure and cut the final red oak facing or wrap that goes on the right side of the core assembly. It is 5½" × 38½". Attach it using countersunk screws and glue. Fill the holes with wood plugs, and sand it flush.

I installed a piece of ¾" plywood in the bottom of the inside area of the frame. This is not listed in the materials list because it is an option; many of you will undoubtedly want to install drawers or maybe some racks for storage of pipe clamps or whatever. If you are not that motivated, the piece of plywood is 32" × 60" with notches cut into the ends to fit around the base posts.

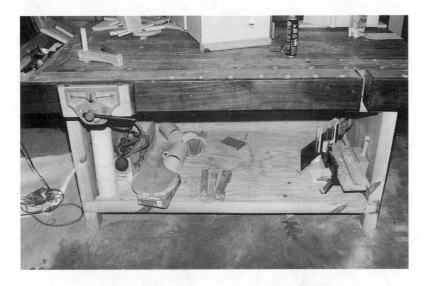

The steps from here on are a tad bit more difficult than the first steps of this operation because you are now going to install the end vice hardware. There are two versions available: One is 14" and another 17". I used the 14" model because I am cheap and did not want to spend the difference for the larger model. I couldn't see what the difference in cost would buy me. Also, if you are clever with

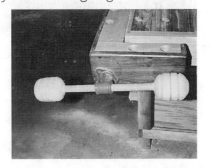

The ultimate workbench 113

inventions and such, you can take the basic ideas from chapter 13 and make your own end vice using wood or polycarbonate materials instead of steel hardware.

The basic components that make up an end vice are the screw, the upper and lower guide plates, the bench plate, the bench screw sleeve, and the nuts and bolts that hold it all together. What we are going to do is essentially build a box around these components, attach them to the side of the workbench, and then build up the sides, tops, and backs that make up the external appearance of the end vice.

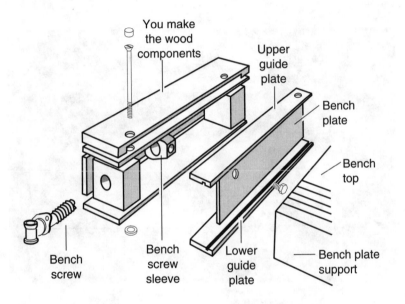

You make the wood components

Upper guide plate

Bench plate

Bench top

Bench plate support

Lower guide plate

Bench screw sleeve

Bench screw

Supply information

I purchased the hardware that I used at Wood-craft Supply, a large mail-order house with stores in many cities. Their address is:

> 210 Wood County Industrial Park
> Box 1686
> Parkersburg, West Virginia 26102-1686

There are many other fine woodworking stores located all across the country, and you can find the components for this vice at any number of different locations. A good source for them is woodworking magazines. Most of the larger mail-order houses run ads that will tell you how to contact them.

Step 1

I did not have a guidebook to tell me how to do this, so I am going to tell you the way I did it. There might be simpler steps; I simply do not know of any. First, measure and cut a piece of hardwood on which to mount the bench plate. You want to mount the bench plate so that there is adequate room for the upper and lower guide plates to move back and forth and not touch the sides of the bench top. At the same time, you want them to be close enough so that you can build up the wood components so the exterior of the end vice looks like it is right next to the bench top.

The bench plate support is ½" × 3" × 12". Mount this on the end of the bench top, 1" from the end and 1½" from the top of the bench top. Use countersunk screws and glue.

Step 2

Mount the bench plate to the bench plate support so that it is 1" from the end of the bench top and 1¼" from the top of the bench top. You will have to drill a hole for the bench-screw-sleeve nut that fits on the back of the bench plate so that the whole assembly can be mounted flush.

The ultimate workbench 115

Step 3 Measure and cut the core pieces that form the box on which the guideplates are attached. The end pieces are 3¹⁄₁₆" high × 2¾" wide, while the bottom and top boards are 2" × 16⅛". Glue these boards together as shown. Wait until the glue is dry before proceeding.

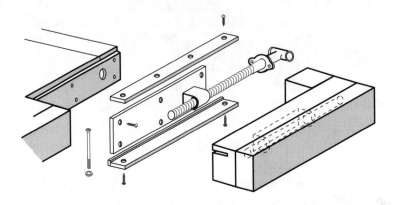

Step 4 Mount the guideplates on top of the core using clamps to hold them in place. Slide the whole contraption onto the bench plate. See if it glides back and forth with ease. There should be no movement up and down and it should be snug—not tight or loose. You might have to shim the guideplates or sand down the core a little so that they are positioned properly.

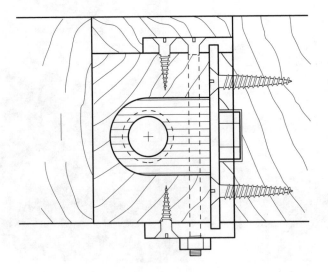

Mark the center position for the bench screw sleeve onto the end of the forward end piece. Dismantle the whole configuration. Using the center mark on the end board, drill a hole slightly larger than the diameter of the metal screw that you purchased with the end vice kit.

Reassemble the core and the guideplates and attach them using the nuts and bolts provided with the end vice kit. In my case, the lower guide plates were tapped for the bolt and I did not need a nut; however, for insurance, I added one nut to the inside of the assembly so that I knew that I had a solid and firm assembly.

At this point, you can start building up the basic exterior of the end vice. I opted to simply add one board on top of the whole assembly that was 3¾" × 16¼" and then added layers of 12"-long boards forming the L of the end vice. I then wrapped the whole thing with walnut boards.

I use some half-inch Cocobola left over from another project for the faces of the end of the vice. The size is 4½ × 3¾". I had to cut the face of the vice with a notch so that it would glide past the bench plate assembly.

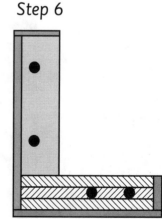

The ultimate workbench 117

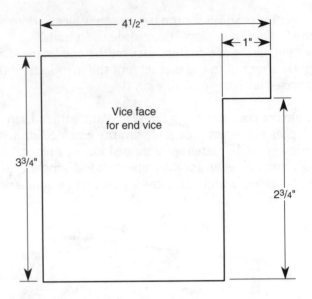

Vice face
for end vice

4¹/₂"

1"

3³/₄"

2³/₄"

Step 7   The final step is to attach the bench screw to the end vice assembly. Attach it to the last piece of walnut wrap using screws.

For the face of the record vice, I used a piece of red oak with a matching piece of walnut on the inside. I routed the edges, but you can round them or leave them just plain square.

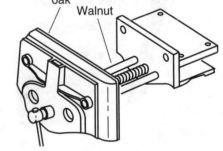

Red oak

Walnut

Finishing touches   I routed the outside edge of the workbench top and the inside of the tool crib area with a router and a rounding over bit.

I added a variety of 1" holes in the bench top, as you can see from the photos. Depending on the kinds of bench dogs you want to use, make the necessary holes to fit those. Make certain that you carefully align the holes in the vice faces with the holes in the workbench top. They must be drilled at exact distances from one another or they won't work.

I sealed the whole project with a Danish-oil product, giving it several coats over a period of two weeks.

For those of you who dream about having your own workbench and were just intimidated to death with the ultimate workbench, I have a simpler, easier-to-construct project. This is called the 2 × 4 workbench and it can be made over a weekend with a minimum of tools—and you can still use the record vice at least, or the one from chapter 14. It is 3'× 6' and is about 36" tall. It also includes a lower shelf. It has no built-in features such as bench dogs, vices, or hold-downs, but you can refer to other pages in this book for information on how to build these additions.

2×4 workbench

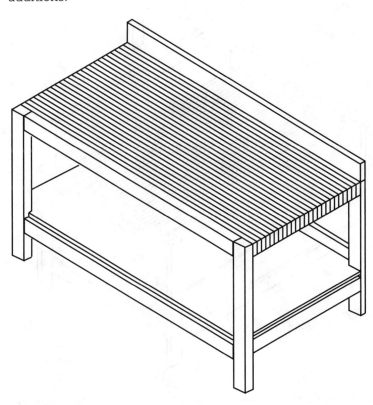

Step 1 Measure and cut all of the wood pieces per the materials list. The parts marked A are screwed and glued, along with the parts marked C, to form the bench top. I suggest that you clamp the boards together to make certain the surface is smooth, putting about four screws into each board. I also suggest that if you intend to drill holes in the bench later on, you should make a line on the bottom so as to show where you put the screws. Try to keep the screws within an inch of each other straight across the width of the bench top.

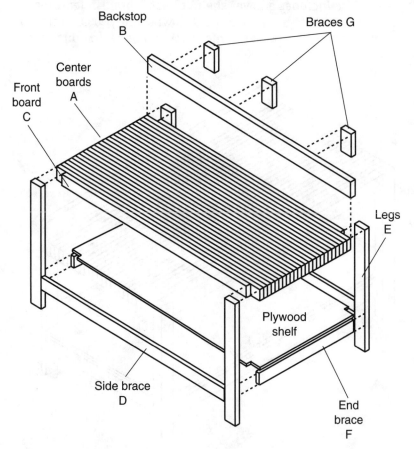

Measure and cut four V-wedges out of 2 × 4 stock to strengthen the side and end braces.

Install the legs flush with the bench top. I suggest that you do this with the bench top upside-down on a flat surface. Next, attach the side and end braces to the legs using V-wedges to strengthen the joints.

Step 2

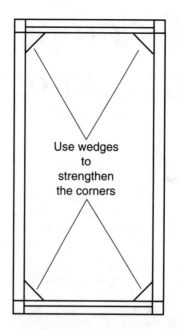

Use wedges
to
strengthen
the corners

Measure and cut the plywood shelf and insert it into the opening underneath the top. Attach the three braces to the back of the back stop, and attach this assembly to the top of the workbench.

Step 3

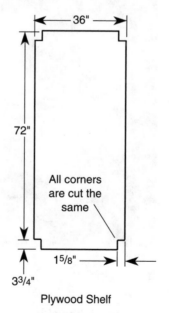

36"

72"

All corners
are cut the
same

15/8"

3³/4"

Plywood Shelf

Seal the surface of the workbench with a good tung-oil or Danish-oil sealer. Then go find something to make with your new workbench!

Step 4

C clamps &
bar clamps

THESE PROJECTS UTILIZE an inexpensive carriage bolt with nuts and lock washers and some wood scraps to form some really practical and useful shop tools. You can never have enough clamps and, with this technique, you can make as many as you need—for peanuts compared to the store bought kind. These clamps differ from other cam-type clamps in that you can bring more pressure to bear on the project that you are joining or gluing up. Each type of clamp has its application, but these are a little more flexible.

Materials

(For C-clamps)
1" red oak ½ board foot
   1 piece 6" × 8"
½" Baltic birch 1 board foot

2 pieces 6" × 8"
(For bar clamp)
½" Baltic birch scraps from above
  2 pieces 1½" × 4½" fixed jaw
  2 pieces 1½" × 5" adjustable jaw
1" × 1½" red oak 22"
  1 piece 16" bar
  1 piece 3" fixed jaw
  1 piece 2¼" top of adjustable jaw
  1 piece 1" bottom of adjustable jaw

1 carriage bolt ⅜" × 6" with 2
  matching nuts and lockwashers
(For each clamp)
1" hardwood scraps
2 pieces ⅛" square metal bar
Stock 2" long
Carpenter's glue
Epoxy

Saber saw
Drill with ⅜", ⅛" and ½" bits
Router with rounding over bit
Pad or belt sander

Measure and cut the three pieces that will form the C-clamp sandwich. Cut the ends from the outside Baltic birch plywood sides and the inner red oak piece, where indicated. Glue all of these pieces to form a sandwich—one the main clamp the other the end pieces.

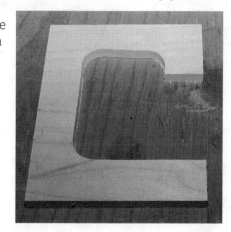

C clamps & bar clamps 123

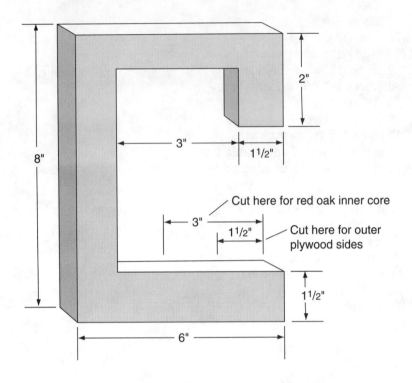

8"

2"

3"

1¹/₂"

Cut here for red oak inner core

3"

1¹/₂"

Cut here for outer plywood sides

1¹/₂"

6"

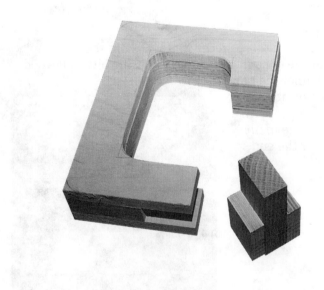

124 Workshop accessories you can make

Center and drill a slightly elongated, ⅜" hole in the end-pieces assembly. You want the carriage bolt to fit loosely in this hole.

Center one of the nuts over the ⅜" hole and chisel out a recess for the nut to fit into. Insert a carriage bolt to make certain the opening is proper and that the carriage bolt can turn, then glue the nut into position using epoxy. (Be very careful to not get any epoxy on the nut or on the carriage bolt threads or you will be very upset with yourself later!) Next, grind the head of the carriage bolt flat.

Cut two small 1¼" circles from the scrap hardwood: one ⅜" thick and one 1" thick from the scrap hardwood. (I used walnut.) Center and drill a ½" hole through the center of the smaller block of wood. Next drill a ¾" hole, centered, halfway through the other block. Place the head of the bolt through these pieces and glue them closed.

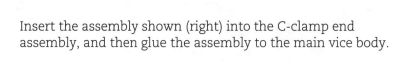

Insert the assembly shown (right) into the C-clamp end assembly, and then glue the assembly to the main vice body.

C clamps & bar clamps 125

Step 5 From the ½" Baltic birch scrap, measure and cut the piece that will form the handle. The form this takes is up to you, but it should be comfortable for your hand. The handle shown here is but one option. It is 3" × 3".

Drill a ⅜" hole into the center of this handle and attach it to the end of the carriage bolt using nuts and lock washers.

Step 6 Using a router with a rounding-over bit, soften the sides of the clamp to eliminate splinters and to make the project easy to handle. Then sand it all over.

Bar clamp The bar clamp is made just a little differently, but it has the same type of clamping mechanism. The main difference is that the sliding adjustable jaw gives you further flexibility in clamping odd sizes.

Step 1 Measure and cut to size the 1" oak and ½" Baltic birch pieces that go to make up the fixed jaw. Then glue the three fixed jaw pieces together; do not attach them to the bar yet.

When the glue has dried, center and drill a ⅜" hole into the center of the wood sandwich or assembly just as in the case of the C-clamp. Chisel out the provision for the nut, and epoxy it in place.

Step 2

Next, follow the same procedure for making the clamp-face assembly with handle. Glue the fixed jaw into position on the wood bar with the nut on the inside.

Step 3

Step 4   Attach the clamp face assembly to the fixed-jaw end of the bar clamp. As you can tell from the photo, I made a modified version of the original handle. Use ½" Baltic birch plywood for this step. Attach the handle to the threaded shaft using two lock washers and nuts, and clamp it securely.

Step 5   The adjustable jaw is made by sandwiching the plywood and the oak pieces so that the wood bar rides through the opening between the two oak pieces, which are flanked by the plywood sides. Additionally, the use of a metal bar helps to grip the bar when force is exerted upon the adjustable jaw assembly.

This step is one you will have to complete carefully. Drill two holes where the drawing indicates using a ⅛" bit. Drill evenly, absolutely straight down.

Measure and cut the two ⅛" bar stock pieces to a length of 2". Sharpen one end with a point using a grinder or sander.

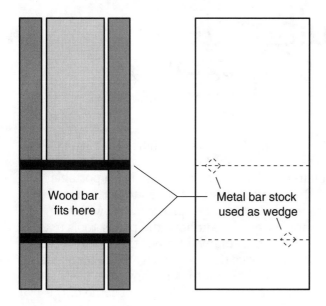

Wood bar fits here

Metal bar stock used as wedge

Next, using a hammer, tap the metal bars into place. It is important that the edge of the bar be down and upward so that when the jaw is tilted against the work, the bars dig into the wood bar—thus holding the project securely and not slipping under the pressure of the tightened clamp. Sand the metal bars flush with the sides of the adjustable jaw. Finally, slip the adjustable jaw over the end of the wood bar.

The ultimate "work horse"

THE ULTIMATE WORK HORSE IS a saw horse that is a tad bit more complicated then the old-fashioned ones you are probably familiar with. This one can be used as a portable workbench on the job site. It can allow you to perform an enormous number of work tasks. It provides you with the ability to use many different handheld and power tools in a variety of forms to perform many different tasks, and it even allows you to do some tasks normally relegated to large, stand-alone power tools. While the photo here shows the basic lower frame, this chapter also gives you a glimpse of some of the things that this project gives you the power and ability to perform.

2 × 4 pressure-treated lumber 24 linear feet
  2 pieces 14" top ends
  2 pieces 51" top sides
  1 piece 51" lower center support
  2 pieces 18" lower ends
  2 pieces 19" slanted center supports
  4 pieces 34" legs
2 pieces ¾" plywood 23½" × 60" work surface
1 × 6 pine or fir 60"
  2 pieces 1½" × 25" work surface ends
  2 pieces 1½" × 60" work surface sides
1 × 8 fir or pine 60"
  8 pieces 6" jaw faces
  8 pieces 2½" jaw face supports

Materials

Carpenter's glue
40 Dacrotized screws 2½"
20 Dacrotized screws 1½"
Clear silicone sealant / glue
4 carriage bolts ½" × 7" with nuts and lock washers
8 pieces wood dowel ¾" × 8"
Baltic birch plywood scraps ½"

Hardware & miscellaneous

Circular saw
Drill with countersink, ½" & ¾" bits
Screwdriver
Saber saw
Router with rounding-over bit
Square
Protractor
Clamps

Tools required

Step 1 Measure and cut the 2×4 pieces forming the upper or top portion of the saw horse. You will need two 14" pieces and two 51" pieces. Next, measure and cut the leg pieces. They are 34" long and cut at a 15-degree slant on each end.

Assemble the top portion by screwing the ends to the sides using 2½ Dacrotized screws, countersunk, and silicone sealant.

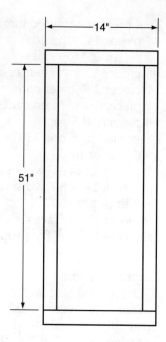

Step 2 Attach the legs to the top assembly as shown in the diagram. Again, use countersunk screws and silicone sealant.

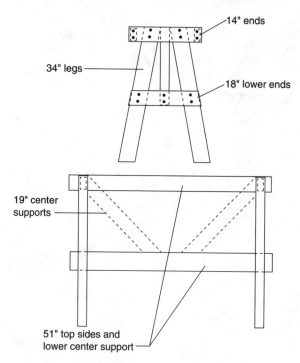

Next, measure and cut the lower center support board (51"). Cut the lower ends at a 15-degree angle, 18" at the longest end. Then cut the center-slanted support boards at a 45-degree angle.

Attach the lower side boards to the legs about 19" from the floor. Center the lower-center support board on the lower side boards, then finish off with the center-slanted support boards. Cut the top end off these boards to fit flush with the top of the 2 × 4 edge of the top assembly. Countersink 2½" Dacrotized screws and use silicone sealant.

Step 4 At this juncture, you have your basic saw horse frame. There are a number of attachments that can go onto it at this point, but let's start with the basic benchtop or worksurface. I made two tops. One is 1" thick and one is 1½" thick. For now, let's stick with the thicker version.

Measure and cut the plywood pieces, 2 pieces ¾" plywood 23½ × 60".

Step 5 Glue the two pieces of plywood together using carpenter's wood glue. Drive four temporary finishing nails in the corners to register the assembly and hold it together. Clamp the wood securely with anything you can get your hands on: Drive the car on top of it or use sand bags, but do not use screws or nails.

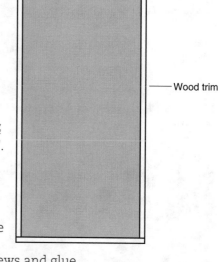
Wood trim

Measure and cut the pine trim pieces. The ends are 1½ × 25", and the sides 1½" × 60".

After the assembly has set up, remove the temporary finishing nails. Attach the wood trim to the sides of the plywood top using 1½" countersunk Dacrotized screws and glue.

Now you have a basic worksurface. You can center and attach it to the base assembly, or you can do more to it. (Read on!)

Bench dogs In order to use bench dogs or cam dog clamps (see project 1), you need to drill holes into the surface to accommodate them. Such clamps are excellent add-ons for holding work in place. The illustration shows a suggested pattern of 1" holes to accommodate these devices. Make certain to avoid drilling into the base frame below. By attaching a vice at one end that aligns with these holes, you can clamp and work with a wide variety of projects.

NOTE: In addition to cam dog clamps and bench dogs, there are a variety of cams and hold-down devices that you can dream up on your own. By attaching clamps to the sides and ends of this basic saw horse, you can hold boards for sawing and planing. In addition, these same clamps can also be used to hold other devices as well as the above benchtop in place.

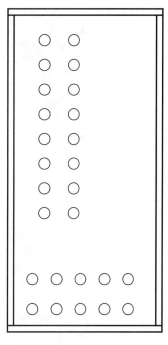

Holes are 6" apart

By using ordinary, store-bought nuts and bolts, you can make some attachments that are very useful.

Measure and cut some 1 × 8 material into 6" and 2½" strips to make the pictured vices. Measure and cut 8" lengths of ¾" wood dowels for guides.

Simple vices

Step 1

The ultimate "work horse" 135

Step 2 Assemble the vices by gluing the short piece to the longer piece as shown. When the glue is dry, drill two ¾" holes as shown and a ½" hole in the center for the carriage bolt.

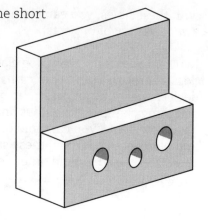

Step 3 Chisel out a recess in the back of one of the assemblies to contain either a nut or a wing nut. Epoxy the nut in place.

Next, cut a handle from some ½" Baltic birch, drill a ½" hole in the center, and attach it to the carriage bolt using a nut and lock washer.

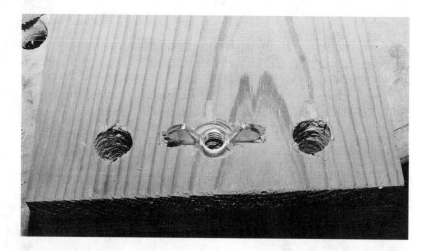

Step 4 Cut a slit in the ends of the wood dowels. Insert them into the front jaw and glue them in place. Tap some scrap wood V-wedges into the slits, forcing the dowels to fit tight in the jaw. When the glue has dried, cut the wedges off flush and sand the face of the jaw.

Insert the whole assembly into the back jaw and attach the carriage bolt assembly by screwing through the front jaw into the nut in the back of the back jaw. This will allow you to move the front jaw forward. When opening the jaw, you will have to pull it out manually as you turn the carriage bolt assembly.

I made four of the vices just described and attached them flush with the top of the sides at each end. This application makes them ideal for planing.

I added some 2" wood strips to the bottom of the plywood top so the vices could hold it in place and so they could be used in conjunction with the bench dogs.

Vice applications

To do this, measure and cut the back vice jaw 2" shorter than the front jaw and mount the vice to the side or ends of the plywood top so that the back jaw is flush with the top or surface. This means there is 2" of the front jaw that is higher than the top.

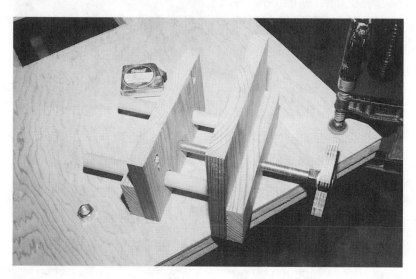

Saw/router additions

You can cut out a recess in the plywood top for a router and saber saw insert.

Step 1

First, measure and cut a 7½"-square hole in the center end of the plywood top. In my example, I cut a slightly rounded edged hole 18" from one end of the plywood top in the center.

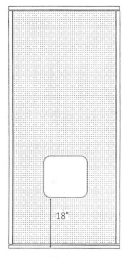

Location of insert cutout

Rout a ¼"-deep and ½"-wide rabbet around the edge of the hole. Then measure and cut a piece of a ¼"-thick polycarbonate, 8½" square.

Step 2

Remove the router base plate from the router that you intend to mount on the polycarbonate and center it on the polycarbonate plate. Mark the location of the holes for the center of the base as well as the screw holes' positions.

Drill countersunk holes for the mounting screws and a hole large enough in the center for the router bits to fit without touching the sides of the polycarbonate. A 2" hole should be sufficient. However, if you intend to use a template guide or insert, make it that size. The standard for a Porter Cable insert is 1¼".

Step 3

Mount the router to the polycarbonate sheet and insert it into the cutout. As a word of precaution, I suggest that you cut the polycarbonate sheet first and use it as a template when marking the cutout for the insert in the plywood top.

Cut a 2×4 to the width of the plywood top and use it as a fence for the router by clamping it to the tabletop. You can also use one of the other fence designs shown in other chapters.

You can make any number of
variations to the applications
suggested in this chapter. The
"Work Horse" is intended as a
work tool that you take to the
job site. The flexibility that you
wish to design into your version
is limited only by your
imagination.

Dream on

Chop saw & panel-cutting jig

THIS PROJECT ENABLES YOU TO attach your circular saw to a panel of polycarbonate and insert it into this slider jig that will allow you to do all of the functions of a chop saw and many of the functions of both a table saw and a radial-arm saw. In addition, it allows you to cut 4 × 8 sheets of plywood or paneling, either cross-cutting or ripping. It mounts on top of the "Work Horse" and can easily be transported to the work site.

Materials

1 piece ¾" plywood 23½" × 60" work surface
1 piece ¼" plywood 23½" × 60" work surface
1 × 6 pine or fir 15 linear feet
   2 pieces 1" × 25" work surface ends
   2 pieces 1" × 60" work surface sides
   2 pieces 2¼" × 57" runner tops
   2 pieces 1½" × 57" runner bottoms
   1 piece 2" × 33" short fence
   1 piece 2" × 69" long fence
   4 pieces 2" × 4" fence stops
   4 pieces 3" × 5" fence lock
   4 pieces 1" × 3" fence lock pivots
2 × 4 pine or fir 3 linear feet
   4 pieces 4½" × 4½" × 6" runner supports

Carpenter's glue
20 Dacrotized screws 1½"
4 carriage bolts ¼" × 4" with wing nuts and washers
6 flat-headed stove bolts ¼" × 2" with two wing nuts
Baltic birch plywood scraps ½"
2 pieces steel bar stock ⅛" × 1" × 57"
1 piece polycarbonate ¼" × 14" square

Circular saw
Drill with countersink, ⅛" & ½" bits
Screwdriver
Saber saw
Square
Clamps

Step 1

Measure and cut the two plywood pieces. Glue the two pieces of plywood together using carpenter's wood glue. Drive four temporary finishing nails in the corners to register the assembly and to hold it together. Clamp the wood securely with anything EXCEPT screws or nails.

While the glue is drying, measure and cut the pine trim pieces. The ends are 1" × 25" and the sides 1" × 60".

After the assembly has set up, remove the temporary finishing nails. Attach the wood trim to the sides of the plywood top using 1½" countersunk Dacrotized screws and glue. At this juncture you have your basic work surface.

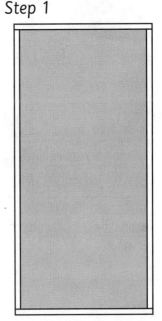

Wrap the ends and
sides with 1" wood strips

Cut a 5/16" deep and 5/8"
wide dado or slot into the
bottom runner as shown.

Step 2

Measure and cut the top and bottom runner pieces. Cut a 5/16" deep and ⅝" wide dado or slot into the bottom runner as shown.

Step 3 Measure and cut the steel bar to a length of 57". You will need a hacksaw for this purpose, unless you can talk the people at the home-supply center into cutting it for you.

Drill ⅛" holes into ¼" space every 6". Using a ½" bit, drill a slight countersink on top of the ⅛" holes as a countersink for the screw heads. Attach the top and bottom runners as shown.

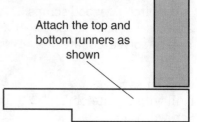

Attach the top and bottom runners as shown

Step 4 Attach the metal bar onto the bottom runner using ¾" wood screws.

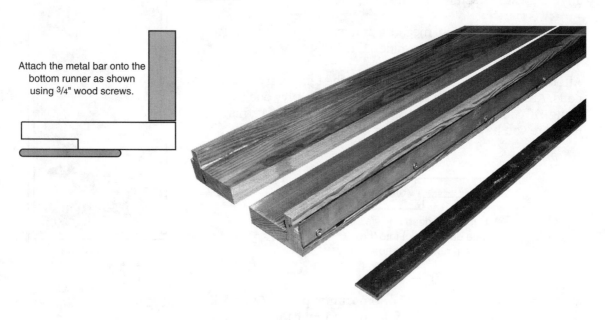

Attach the metal bar onto the bottom runner as shown using 3/4" wood screws.

Measure and cut the four runner support boards from the 2 × 4 stock. Measure and cut the polycarbonate into a 14"-x-14" piece.

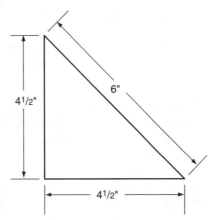

Center and attach the runner supports and the runners onto the work surface, using the polycarbonate sheet as a spacing device. You want the piece to slide forward and backward without binding or right-and-left movement.

This step is absolutely crucial. Set the runners on top of 2 × 4 scraps so that you know that the distance from the work surface to the bottom of the metal bar is 1½. The runners must be absolutely square to the work surface with no skew.

Step 7 Position the circular saw of your choice onto the polycarbonate sheet. Center the saw and square it to the polycarbonate sheet. This step is important because the saw must be absolutely square on the polycarbonate sheet.

Step 8 Carefully mark the outline of the circular saw shoe or base onto the paper or plastic protective covering of the polycarbonate. Mark the area of the saw that contains the protective guard.

Using a drill and a ½" bit, drill a starter hole. Then, with a saber saw, cut out the area marked.

Drill four ¼" holes into the shoe or base of the saw, two in front and two in the back of the plate. Make certain you do not drill in an area that will affect any of the components of the saw or attachments.

Reposition the saw on the polycarbonate and mark onto the polycarbonate sheet the location of the four holes in the plate or base of the saw. Again, remember the saw must be exactly square on the polycarbonate.

From the opposite side, drill four countersunk holes into the polycarbonate with a ¼" bit and a countersink at the marked locations. I elected to tap the metal plate or base of the saw to receive the screws that I used, but that is an option. You can simply use nuts and lock washers to do the same thing. In any event, attach the saw to the polycarbonate sheet again checking to make certain it is square.

Slide the saw/polycarbonate assembly into the runners and
check to make certain it rides smoothly without any rocking
motion and that there is no slack or wobbling in the runner or
guide.

Measure and cut four pieces of ½" Baltic birch into two pieces
1" × 1¾" and two into ½" × 1". Glue the pieces together as shown.
These will form locking mechanisms
to hold the saw in position when
making rip cuts.

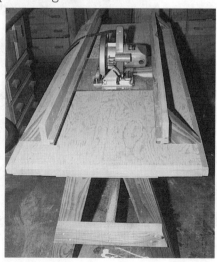

Attach the two assemblies to the
polycarbonate as shown. Drill a hole
through the locking mechanisms
and the polycarbonate on the edge
so that the locking mechanism can
clamp to the top of the bottom
runner. I suggest that you glue a
small strip of sandpaper to the lip of
the mechanism so that it can grip
the runner tightly and securely.

Chop saw & panel-cutting jig 147

Step 11 The saw can now be placed into two different positions in the runner assembly. You can cut plywood and regular boards in both directions. Using a standard 7½" saw, you can cut up to 1½"-thick lumber. You can also make compound miter cuts up to 40 degrees. For a 45-degree cut you must raise the work by about ¼" from the work surface. If you use an 8" circular saw this will not be necessary.

NOTE: In some cases, you want your hands free and the saw locked into position so that you can feed the work into the saw. If your saw is not equipped with a switch lock, you will have to wire it into the on position. If you elect to do this, I strongly suggest that you wire an on/off switch somewhere on the jig assembly so that the saw can be plugged into an outlet and turned on at the switch location. If you do not know how to do this, find a friend who knows basic electrical wiring.

The next step is to make the fences. There are three fences for this jig: one for the rip-assembly position, one for the crosscut-assembly position, and one for miter and angle cutting.

Making the fences

The angle-cutting fence is for use with the saw in a crosscut position. It is adjustable to various angles and pivots from a pin position on the work surface near the saw blade.

The pivoting fence is cut 20" long and 2" wide. It is rounded at one end so that it can pivot near the blade of the saw but not touch it. This is accomplished with the use of a ½" wooden dowel inserted into the work surface. It has a 6" × ½" slot cut in

Pivoting fence

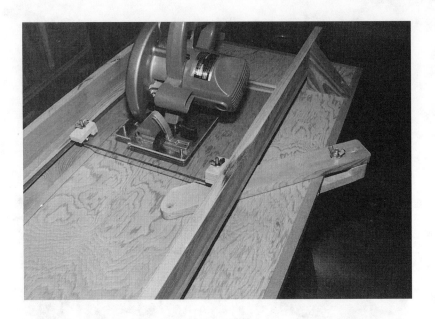

the center at one end so that a sliding clamping mechanism can be used to hold it securely to the work surface at any angle.

The clamping mechanism is 2" × 7" with a 2" × 1" × 1" block on the end. A ½" × 3" carriage bolt is inserted at one end and the whole thing is clamped to the work surface with a washer and wing nut. A ½" wooden dowel is attached to the end of the block to guide the clamping mechanism in the slot.

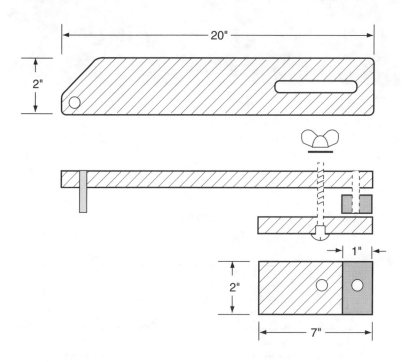

20"

2"

1"

2"

7"

Chop saw & panel-cutting jig 151

Crosscut & rip fences

The next two fences are identical except for length. They are designed to serve as a guide for the work either in crosscut or rip operations. The crosscut fence is 69" long, while the rip fence is 33" long. They are 2" wide with 2" × 4" stops at each end designed to keep them at a perfect 90-degree angle to the saw blade. Rocking-clamping mechanisms lock the fences into position on the work surface.

Measure and cut all of the fence components. Position the stops at each end, square everything to the work surface, and attach the stops using countersunk screws and glue. This step is crucial because the fence should immediately square to the saw blade when dropped into position thus the stops must be snug at the ends.

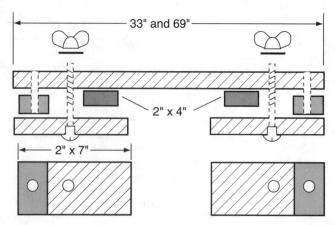

Hold downs and other devices are a must when using this jig. Fingerboards and accordion boards are devices that can be clamped to the jig or work surface and hold work into position. Since the very nature of the saw rotation will pull the work up, something must hold the work down. Likewise when feeding the work alongside a fence something must hold the work against the fence. Using your hands to do this could be dangerous.

Hold-downs & other devices

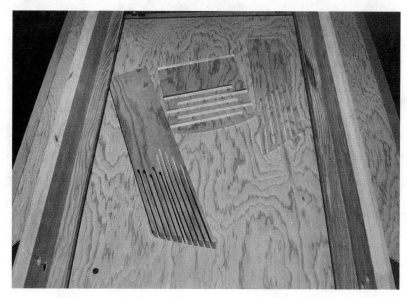

Fingerboards should be made from a hardwood with the fingers cut with the grain of the wood. They can be clamped to the work surface with the use of clamps or you can make an assembly as shown.

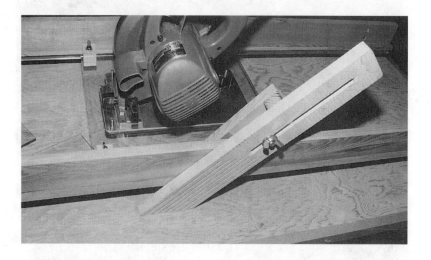

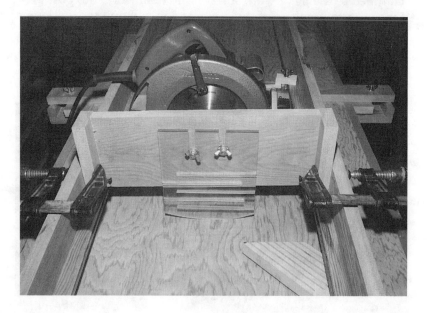

Accordion pressure boards should be made from either plywood or a polycarbonate material. You can buy spring hold-downs at woodworking stores, but the kind you make yourself are the least expensive.

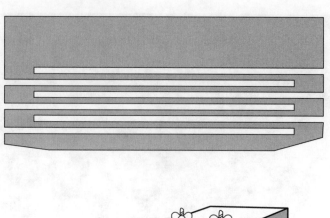

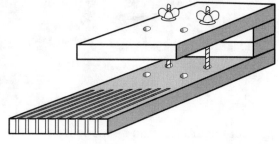

Portable workbench

Tʜɪs PORTABLE WORKBENCH-AND-CLAMP COMBINATION is very inexpensive and fairly easy to make. Best of all, you can take it on the back porch, into the yard or garage, or to the lake house on a weekend. It is 12" wide and 32" long, with a 12" vice jaw that can open to over 10". You can easily clamp it to any table or bench top. It is made from common items you can buy at any home center or hardware store. When used in conjunction with bench dogs and other types of hold downs it is a very useful item to have around the house.

1 × 8 red oak 8 linear feet
  2 pieces 6" × 30" top
  2 pieces 4" × 28½" sides
  2 pieces 4" × 12" ends
  2 pieces hidden vice parts
  3 pieces 4" × 12" vice jaw
  1 piece 2¼" × 12" vice top
  5 pieces 3" diameter jaw handle hub

Materials

8 pieces 2" diameter handle ends
4 pieces 2" square stops

Hardware & miscellaneous

2 pieces wood dowel ¾" × 16" vice guides
1 piece wood dowel ¾" × 18" handle
4 pieces 1" wood dowel stops
1 piece threaded metal rod ⅝" × 16" vice screw with 3 nuts and two lockwashers
1 washer 1¼" diameter
1 washer with ¾" hole
1 piece polycarbonate ¼" × 1¼"
Carpenter's glue
20 drywall screws 1½"

Tool required

Drill with ⅝", ¾" 1", 1¼" and countersink bits
Circular saw
Saber saw
Belt sander
Screwdriver
Hammer
Tape measure
Router with rounding-over bit
Single-cut bastard file

Step 1

You are going to make a basic box that has sides, ends, and a top. The top is made from two 6"-wide boards of 30"-long red oak laminated to form one 12"-x-30" piece. The ends are connected to the sides and the top is connected to all of them.

Before connecting all of the pieces, though, you first want to cut all of the pieces that form the vice jaw, then stack them all together and drill three holes in alignment. At this point, then, measure and cut all the pieces and laminate the top.

Next, drill 1" holes into the side boards so that you have a clamping access for holding this project to the surface of whatever it is you plan to construct. I suggest four holes in each side, centered and evenly spaced.

Step 2

Drill two holes 2½" from each end and ⅞ from the bottom, then drill one ⅝" hole in the center, ¾" from the bottom. Be sure you drill into the stack of boards that forming the vice jaws, one end, and the two inside pieces.

Step 3

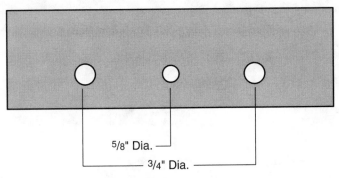

5/8" Dia.

3/4" Dia.

Attach the ends to the sides using glue and countersunk screws. (Remember that the front end is predrilled for the vice assembly.) Then attach the top to the vice-jaw assembly using glue and countersunk screws.

Step 4

This next task is somewhat tedious. Using a file—specifically, a single-cut bastard file—cut a round groove into the threaded steel rod 3" from one end. Reduce the diameter of the rod to ⅜". The width of the groove should be about ⅜".

Step 5

Measure and cut a piece of polycarbonate 1¼" in diameter with a ⅜" hole in the center. Drill a ⅜" hole into the center of the 1¼" washer. Cut the polycarbonate and the washer in half. The easiest way to cut the washer in half is to mount it in a vice

Step 6

and cut a groove in the center with the edge of the file until the groove in the washer is thin enough to snap the washer in two.

Step 7   Drill a 1¼" hole ⅜" deep into the center hole of the center board of the vice jaw assembly. Insert the threaded metal rod into the hole and surround it with the washer and polycarbonate pieces. Sandwich the center board with two other boards, and glue and clamp the assembly. Make absolutely certain that the other two holes are in perfect alignment before proceeding.

Trim the other two vice parts to fit inside of the box (¾" off each end).

Next, center a nut that fits the threaded rod over the center hole of one of the inside boards. Mark the outline with a pencil. Using a chisel, cut out the nut image to a depth of about ⅜". Epoxy the nut into that hole, making certain not to get any epoxy into the center hole nor the nut threads.

Step 8

Place a large washer over the nut you just epoxied, and mark positions for two screws and the end to be trimmed flat. Grind the end flat, and drill the two holes. Then reposition the washer over the nut, and screw it in place with two ¾" drywall screws. Make certain there is adequate room for the threaded rod to screw into the nut and past the washer.

Step 9

Step 10 Glue the board-nut-washer assembly to the inside back of the
end board with the holes in it. Again make absolutely certain
that the holes are all in perfect alignment.

Insert the long end of the threaded-rod-and-vice-jaw assembly
into the end of the box, and screw it until the vice is closed.
Check the bottom of the jaws to see if they drag or clear the
surface that it is on. You might wish to sand the bottom to
provide a little clearance.

Measure and cut the two ¾" wooden dowels to length. Cut ¾" **Step 11**
deep saber-saw kerfs in the center of each end. Cut four ¾"-
wide V-wedges from scrap
wood stock. Insert the dowels
into the vice jaws and the end
inside board. Glue the dowels
in place, and then tap in place
the V-wedges, forcing the
dowels to wedge into the holes
in the vice face and the rear
inside guide board. Allow this
assembly to dry before
proceeding. Then cut the
wedges flush with the surface,
and sand the ends smooth.

Measure and cut the vice-jaw-assembly top board and glue and **Step 12**
clamp in place. Make certain that it is flush with the top of the
box.

Center a nut for the threaded rod
on two of the vice-jaw handle-
shaft assembly pieces and mark
the outline of the nut. Drill a pilot
hole so the blade can get through.
Then, using a chisel or a saber
saw, cut out this opening so that
the nut will fit inside of the round
piece of wood.

Step 13 Start the handle assembly by putting a nut onto the rod. You will have to experiment here. You want the nut to be about ¼" from the front of the face of the vice. Using a hammer and a metal chisel, damage the threads on the rod. Screw the nut into these damaged threads until it gets stuck.

Step 14 Next, place one of the cutout round pieces over that nut and epoxy it in place. Add a second round piece drilled to slip over the rod. Place a lock washer and a nut and tighten this first assembly as tight as you can make it. Place the next circle with the nut cutout over the last nut and epoxy it in place. Screw it to the other round piece with two recessed drywall screws.

Now add each of the remaining round wood pieces using screws and glue. Keep the screws to the outside of the round wood pieces because later you are going to drill a 1" hole through the center of this shaft and you need to avoid hitting those screws and the end of the metal rod.

NOTE: I routed the first and the last round piece with a router and a rounding over bit to soften the appearances.

Step 15 Drill a 1" hole in the handle assembly as shown. (Remember to remember where you put the screws!) Sand the final assembly to remove any rough edges and to compensate for any of the rounded pieces that might have been slightly off.

Cut one of the 1" wooden dowels to a length of about 18".
Measure and cut the eight round wood pieces that will
make up the handle ends.

Step 16

Stack the round pieces four
up, and glue and clamp.
After the glue has dried,
drill a centered, 1" hole into
the ends of this assembly to
a depth of about 2".

Insert the wood dowel into the
handle assembly and add the end pieces by
gluing them in place.

Close the vice jaws tight.
Using a square, mark the
positions on the top of the
vice jaw and the box top to
drill 1" holes for bench dogs. I
made mine about 6" apart on
the vice jaw and then in 5
succeeding rows of two each,
spaced 5" apart.

Step 17

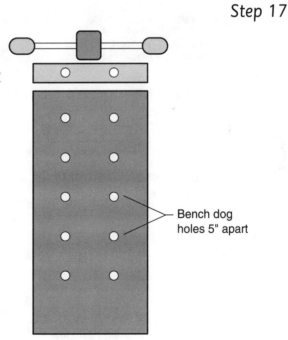

— Bench dog
holes 5" apart

Step 18   Measure and cut the 1" wooden dowels about 4" long for bench dogs. Cut small 2"-square blocks for the bench dog tops. Drill a 1" hole in the center of these blocks, ½" deep. Glue the dowels in place. You will need a minimum of four of these assemblies.

Step 19   Cover all countersunk screw holes with wood plugs and sand flush. Using a router with a rounding-over bit, rout the edges of the bench dog holes and the outside edge of the box and vice-assembly top.

Finally, stain the project the color of your choice.

Drum sander

WHEN WE FIRST LAID OUT the set for the *Weekend Workshop* television show, we decided that a drum sander installed into one of the work surfaces of the U-shaped workshop would be a very functional tool. Drum sanders are easy to make, or you can buy one and install it on a motor. Appliance motors are usually the last thing to go on most washers and dryers, and you can usually pick one up at a garage sale for peanuts. If nothing else, you can buy a refurbished motor for less than the cost of a new one.

Drum sander 167

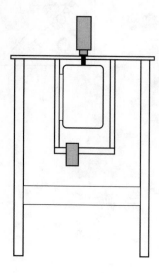

You can mount the drum sander vertically on the surface of the table, as shown (left), which is an ideal position for free-hand shaping. Or you can mount it horizontally on the table (below), which allows you to use the work surface as a fence and to keep the work flat at all times. The fences and other attachments you can make for this sander make a "must-do" project for most workshops.

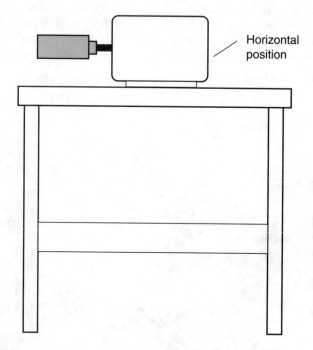

Horizontal position

I used a basic Sears tool motor that was rated at ½ horsepower and 1,750 rpm. Anything faster than that is going to cause wood burn and will burn up your drum sander quickly.

You can mount the motor on the tabletop or underneath it. If you elect to enclose the motor, as I have, you must use a shop vac to remove the sawdust and keep the air circulating around the motor or it will overheat. I installed a piece of 1½" PVC pipe at the bottom of the motor housing for sawdust removal.

The instructions that you are about to read show how to build a basic table for the sander and the housing that surrounds it.

The plywood top is ¾" plywood, with a ¼" Masonite surface. The motor is housed in a box of ¾" plywood, and a piece of ¼" plywood with 2" holes sits on top of the motor to prevent sawdust from entering the motor.

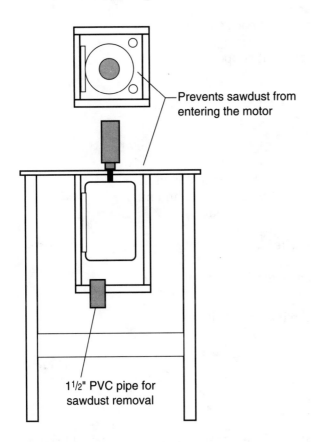

Prevents sawdust from entering the motor

1½" PVC pipe for sawdust removal

Materials

¾" plywood 4 × 4 sheet
  1 piece 8" × 8½" motor housing bottom
  2 pieces 8" × 9" motor housing sides
  2 pieces 7¾" × 9" motor housing ends
  1 piece 18" × 36" table top
  1 piece 7" × 9" fence base
  2 pieces 3" × 4" fence face
1 × 4 pine or fir 5 linear feet
  2 pieces 2" × 8" motor housing supports
  1 piece 2" × 20" miter gauge slot

2 pieces 1" × 37½" table edge trim
2 pieces 1" × 19½" table edge trim ends
¼" Masonite 18" × 36"
2 × 4 fir or pine
    4 pieces 32" table legs
    4 pieces 33" front and back supports
    4 pieces 15" side supports
    4 pieces 45 degree cut supports

Hardware & miscellaneous

3" piece of 1½" PVC pipe
30 wood screws 3"
34 wood screws 1½"
Carpenter's glue
10 wire brads ¾"
2" × 3" sanding drum with ½" shank opening
2 dowel screws ¼" × 3" with washers and nuts
115 volt outlet and box with plate
115 volt switch and box with plate
12 feet 12 gauge wire
½ HP motor 1750 RPM
Book on how to do electrical wiring

Tools required

Drill with countersink and ½" bit
Saber saw
Circular saw
Screwdriver
Hammer
Measuring tape

Step 1

Measure and cut all of the pieces forming the basic table base. Assemble the base using the 2×4 pieces and 3" screws with glue.

Next, measure and cut all of the pieces forming the top. This includes the plywood, the Masonite cover, and the mitered end and front and back trim pieces. Glue the Masonite cover to the plywood, and hold it in place with wire brads. When the glue is dry, add the trim pieces.

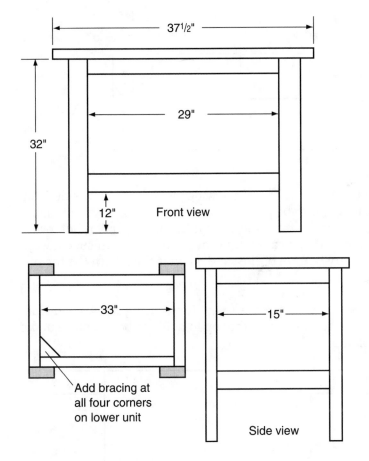

37½"

29"

32"

12"   Front view

33"

15"

Add bracing at
all four corners
on lower unit

Side view

Center the top on the base and attach it using 3" screws at all four corners and in the center of the front and back 2×4 pieces.

Step 2

Measure and cut all of the remaining wood pieces forming the box to house the motor and to hold the miter gauge.

The miter gauge slot is 2" wide and 20" long. It needs to have a slot cut in it to hold the miter gauge you plan to use. In my case, it was a miter gauge from a table saw that required a slot ⅜" deep and ¾" wide.

Step 3

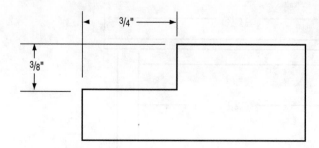

3/4"

3/8"

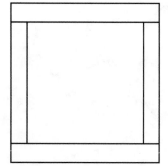

Step 4 Attach the motor to one of the wide pieces of the box side. You want the motor to be positioned so that the shaft will sit high enough about the table top to hold the drum sander, but low enough so that you can mount the drum sander in such a way that the very bottom of the sander rim is flush with the top of the table.

Next, assemble the box pieces as shown using screws and glue. Attach the wood strips at the top to hold the box in place under the tabletop.

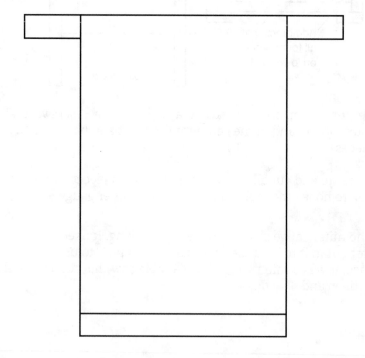

Cut a hole in the bottom of the box to hold the PVC pipe that will be attached to your shop vac to remove sawdust. Glue this PVC pipe in place using silicone caulk/glue.

Step 5

Cut a piece of ¼" plywood to fit over the motor shaft and wedge inside of the top of the box. Cut two 2" holes to the side away from the top of the motor so that the sawdust can flow down and out the PVC pipe. Make certain the hole for the shaft is large enough so that the shaft does not touch the plywood.

Step 6

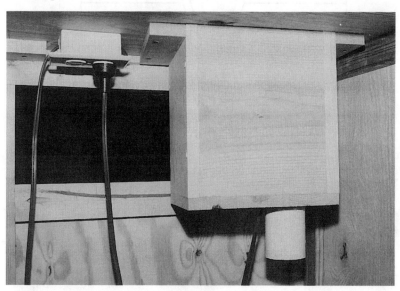

Next, position the hole that you want to make for the drum sander to fit in. I used a 2"-diameter drum sander and cut the hole approximately ¼" wider. Make certain the drum sander you select has a stub end that will fit the shaft of the motor you plan to use.

Attach the motor housing or assembly under the tabletop. Make certain that the sander is centered properly in the hole that you cut. Attach the assembly using screws. I attached the electric cord of the motor to an outlet box that I had wired underneath the tabletop. If you have a basic knowledge of how to do electric wiring you can do the same or find a friend that can help.

Step 7

Step 8 Measure and cut the three remaining wood pieces that form the fence base and faces. The fence base has ¼" slots cut in it to fit around the two dowel screws you must install in the tabletop. A *dowel screw* is a metal rod that has screw threads on one end and machine screw threads on the other end to accept nuts of matching thread size.

The fence faces are attached to the fence base using recessed screws and glue. I formed the inside of the faces by pulling the fence against the drum sander until the sander protruded about ⅛" from the front of the face.

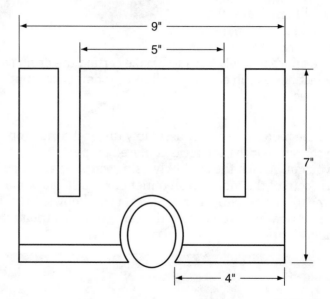

Step 9 Predrill two starter holes and attach the dowel screws behind the sander drum. Attach the fence using nuts and washers. Next, attach the miter gauge board to the side of the table so that the miter gauge is flush with the tabletop. Use screws and glue.

I installed an on/off switch underneath the front ledge of the tabletop I used. This way it is handy for turning the sander off and on. I also had a shop vac underneath the table that automatically turned on when the sander was turned on.

Shooting jig

I CALL THIS A SHOOTING JIG because it allows you to create various cuts in wood that normally would require the use of a table saw. My circular saw shooting jig consists of two L-shaped brackets that fit over the top of a bench vice. Grooves in these brackets hold mating fences or featherboard attachments that can be clamped in place to hold the circular saw on track and can allow you to make very precise cuts in wood. Some of the things the shooting jig can permit you to do include making a groove in a round object (such as a wooden dowel) or perhaps cutting a dado in a small, narrow board. This project truly extends the use of your circular saw.

Materials   1 × 10 red oak hardwood 8 linear feet
2 pieces 6" × 30" tops
2 pieces 3" × 30" bottoms
1 piece 4" × 28" sliding fence
1 piece 3" × 28" finger board fence
3 pieces 3½"× 5" finger boards
6 pieces ¾"× ½" × 3" runners

6 drywall screws 1½"
12 drywall screws 1"
Carpenter's wood glue

Circular saw
Drill with countersink
Router with veining bit
Screwdriver
Clamps
Square

Measure and cut the large wood pieces, and assemble them
using drywall screws.

Step 1

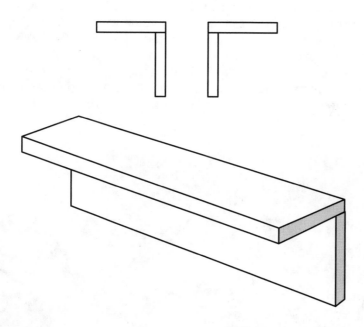

Clamp both assemblies into a vice facing each other, and mark
off the places to cut the grooves. I cut one groove in the center
and the other two 6" to the left and right of center.

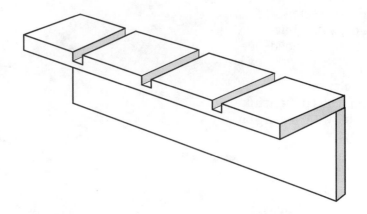

Step 2   Measure and cut the runners. Doing this with a circular saw is a bit tricky; you will need to use the guide with which most circular saws are equipped. I mounted a 5"-wide-x-24"-long piece of oak on-end in the vice. I cut a groove ¾" deep that left a ½" piece on one side and a ⅛" piece on the other side of the groove. I then came back and mounted the board on the side of the workbench, clamped, and cut a ¾"-wide strip to give me the runner sizes I needed. Then I cut them to length, 3".

I made the first fence by inserting the runners into one of the assemblies from step 1 and then put some glue on the runners and then clamped the fence board to the runners, squaring it to the assembly. After the glue dried and the runners were firmly attached, I came back and drilled two countersunk holes into the bottom of the runners and into the fence board and inserted two 1" drywall screws for insurance.

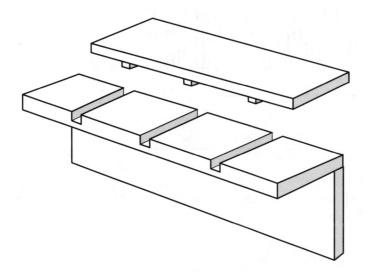

Making the fingerboard fence assembly is a bit more complicated. I cut one of the wide oak boards at a 45-degree angle, then cut slots 2" deep every ¼". I then cut the board to length 3" at a 45-degree angle. I did this a total of three times.

Measure and cut the fingerboard fence, and then cut a dado in one edge, ⅜" deep and ¾" wide, the length of the board. Do the same to the fingerboards.

Step 3

Cut fingerboard fence and
then cut a $3/8$"-deep-x-$3/4$"-wide
dado the length of the board.

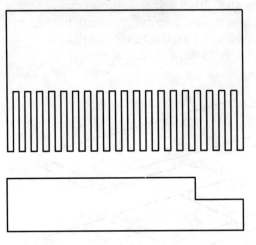

Glue and clamp the finger boards tightly together into the
mating slot of the fence. Repeat the procedure from step 2 for
the runners.

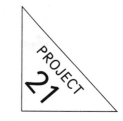

Combination table saw

YOU CAN MOUNT your ordinary handheld circular saw on a piece of polycarbonate so that it can be turned upside-down and inserted into a cutout tabletop. This table project also includes a sliding cut-off jig that allows you to make all kinds of complicated cuts normally requiring a combination of tools. It has a sliding fence that you clamp into position with a cam lock. It also has an extension that you can use for a router table, as well.

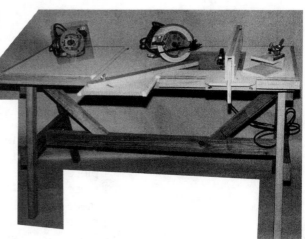

Materials

2×4 pine or fir 24 linear feet
   4 pieces 1½" × 2" × 34" table legs with 75 degree beveled ends
   2 pieces 1½" × 2" × 22" table top frame ends
   2 pieces 1½" × 2" × 57" table top frame sides
   2 pieces 13½" top end leg supports
   2 pieces 22½" middle end leg supports
   1 piece 57" lower stabilizing bar
   2 pieces 22½" end stabilizers
   1 piece 1½" × 1½" × 9½" fence alignment block
   2 pieces ¼" × 1½" × 20" left table lifters
   2 pieces ¼" × 1½" × 26" right table lifters
   1 piece ½" × 1½" × 3½" sliding jig fence

1×6 red oak or equivalent hardwood
   8 linear feet
   2 pieces ⅞" × ¾" × 23" table top end trim
   1 piece ⅞" × ¾" × 26" right table top back trim
   1 piece ⅞" × ¾" × 20" left table top back trim
   2 pieces ⅞" × ¾" 21" left table fence slot guides
   1 piece 2¼" × 21" left table fence slot base

2 pieces ⅞" × ¾" × 26¾" right table fence slot guides
1 piece 2¼" × 26¾" right table fence slot base
1 piece 5" × 26¾" fence center
1 piece ¾" × ¾" × 1¾" fence end lock
1 piece 1⅛" × 6" sliding jig center
1 piece 1" × 3½" sliding jig toggle lock support
1 piece 2" × 25" tilting miter fence

⅞" laminated particleboard top 11 board feet
1 piece 22¼" × 20" left table top
1 piece 11⅞" × 30" sliding table center
1 piece 22¼" × 26" right table top

½" Baltic birch
2 pieces 5" × 26¾" fence sides
1 piece 4" × 9½" fence alignment block top
1 piece 2½" × 8" fence cam
1 piece 2" × 4" fence locking mechanism
1 piece 1¾" × 7¾" fence end
1 piece 6" × 6" sliding jig side
1 piece 3½" × 6" sliding jig side
2 pieces ½" × 1" saw lock
2 pieces 1" × 2" saw lock

Hardware & miscellaneous

1 piece polycarbonate ¼" × 14" × 14" saw base
6 flat head stove bolts ¼" × 1½" with lock washers and wing nuts
30 drywall screws 2½"
30 drywall screws 1¼"
2 thumb screws ¼" × 2" with tee-nuts
Carpenters glue
1 carriage bolt ½" × 2" with wing nut
2 toggle clamps
⅜" wood dowel 1¾"
2 pieces ⅜" wood dowel 1¾" × 2"
2 pieces UHMW plastic ¾" × ⅞" × 30" L bracket
2 pieces UHMW plastic 1¹³⁄₁₆" × 1" × 23¾" U bracket
(NOTE: UHMW is Ultra High Molecular Weight super-slippery plastic. A hardwood may be substituted provided a lubricant such as beeswax is used.)

Drill with countersink and ½" bit
Saber saw
Screwdriver
Circular saw
Router with ½" straight & rabbet bits

Step 1

Measure and cut the wood pieces that form the frame for the tabletop. Attach them as shown using 2½" wood screws as shown below.

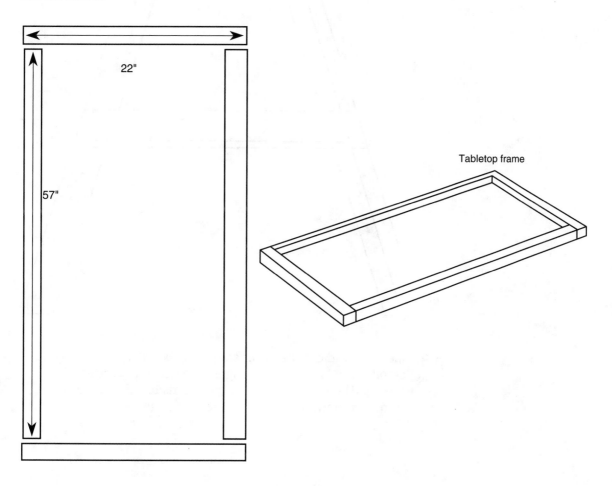

22"

57"

Tabletop frame

Step 2 Measure and cut the pieces that form the legs assemblies. The legs are 34" with 75-degree bevels. Assemble the leg assemblies as shown below.

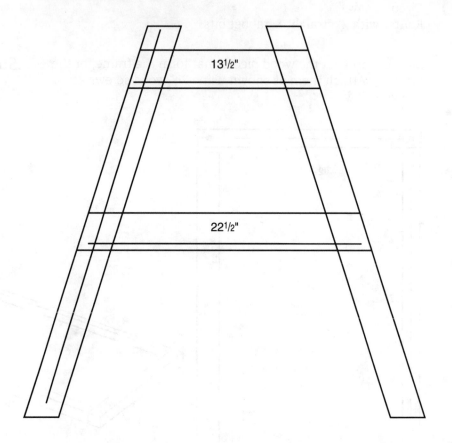

Step 3 Measure and cut the lower stabilizing board and the two end stabilizers. Cut 45-degree angles at each end of the stabilizer boards. Then assemble all of the boards forming the basic frame as shown at the top of the next page.

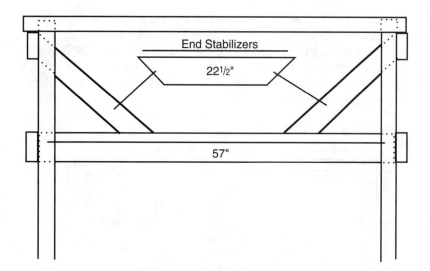

Measure and cut the laminate pieces that will form the top of the table. **Step 4**

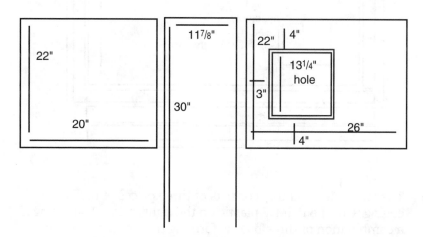

Cut out the square that forms the recess for the circular saw and the polycarbonate base. Note that the hole should be 13¼" with a ⅜"-×-¼" lip forming a 14" insert opening.

Step 5 Measure and cut all of the trim pieces and the UHMW plastic. The plastic should cut just like wood. Start by assembling the lefthand table assembly, where the router cutout is designed to go. While putting a router cutout in this side is an option, a router would increase the flexibility of the project and create a compact power workshop.

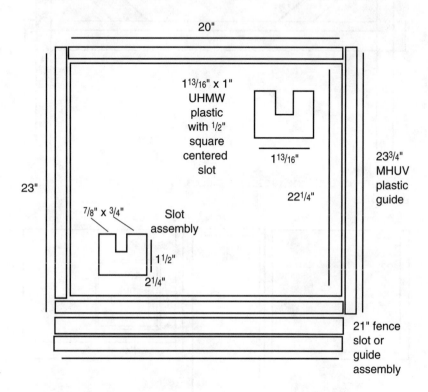

Step 6 The left table assembly consists of three pieces of red oak edging with the UHMW plastic on the right inside. The facing is a combination of three boards forming the slot that the fence will ride in. These are mounted to the edges of the laminate using recessed screws and glue. The best way to attach the U-shaped front slot is to create an L shape first and attach this flush with the top to the front of the left-side assembly. Then add the other board that completes the U-shaped runner. Be certain that the slot is exactly the same width the length of the assembly as shown in the following three illustrations.

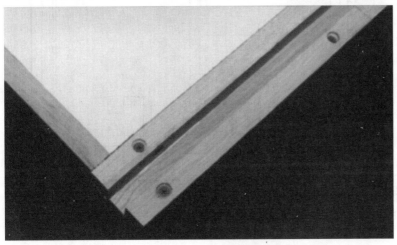

Combination table saw 187

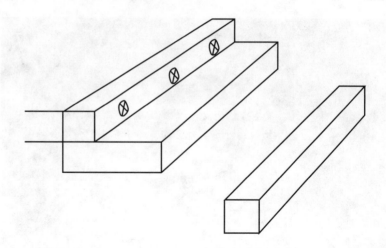

Step 7 Complete the assembly of the right side as shown below and at the top of the next page. Do not attach to the saw frame just yet. Attach the UHMW L-bracket to the sides of the center piece of laminated particleboard. This must be done with precision

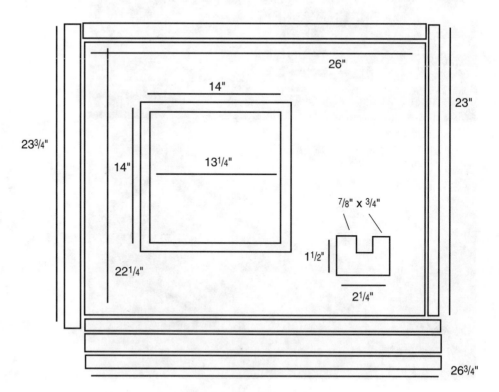

188 Workshop accessories you can make

because the center part must slide easily without binding or side movement. You want the center board to be slightly higher (about 1/64") than the left and right table surfaces.

Step 8 Square the left side of the saw assembly to the left of the saw frame, and clamp it in place on top of the table lifters (strips of 2×4 designed to lift the table top ¼").

Step 9 Slide the left L side of the center board into the U groove of the left tabletop. Next, position the right tabletop into position on top of lifters, and insert the right L side of the center board into the U groove of the right tabletop. Push the right tabletop firmly into the side of the center board, and clamp it in place.

Next move the center board in and out to see if you have a firm and easy glide. There should be no side movement and no binding. You might have to experiment with this several times to get it just right. When you feel that the positioning is correct, screw the left and right side tabletops into the saw frame.

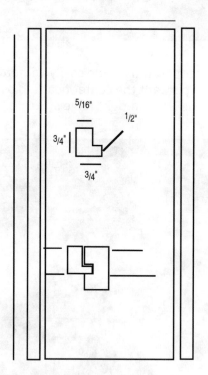

The next step is to create a ½" arc in the center board. There are   **Step 10**
two ways to do this: One with a pattern as a guide as shown
below, and the other using a router with a circle-cutting jig
mounted on the bottom plate as shown at the bottom of the
page. I elected to use the router jig.

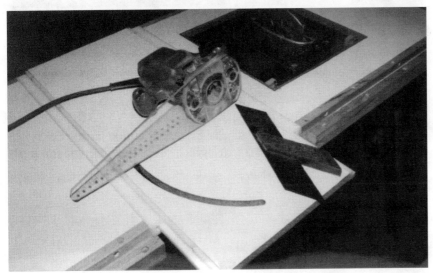

I positioned the router, and then I inserted a screw through the plate and into the table as the center point, which would later serve as a pivot point for a tilting fence. I used a ½" straight pit and gently eased the router into the surface of the center board, cutting ¼" cuts until the slot was cut through the board. Never attempt a cut like this in one pass. Most routers will not have the power to do this job in one pass.

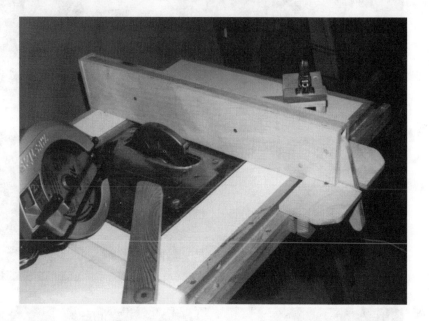

Step 11   Measure and cut the sliding fence and attach it to the sliding center table as shown. Use a washer and screw at the center point and a ½" carriage bolt, 2" long, with a washer and a wing nut.

For insurance, I also installed a toggle locking clamp mechanism to the tilting fence so that I could clamp my work securely when putting it through the saw as shown at the top of the next page.

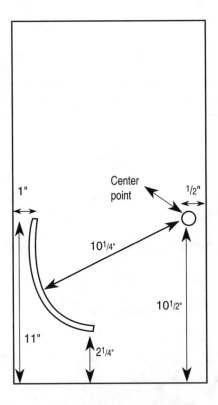

The next step is to cut the pieces forming the cam lock fence. This step takes time and thought. You must create a unit that firmly locks into the groove or slot in the front of the saw table. This is done by the use of a cam and a locking lever. If you can't get this right, don't use it. Clamping a 2×4 to the table will serve the same purpose, provided you get it square.

Step 12

Central to the cam locking device is an assembly with two ¼" thumb screws and tee-nuts that allows you to position the whole fence assembly square to the table. It is called the fence alignment block as shown on the next page. It along with a cam action holds the fence square to the table—provided, of course, that you made it right to begin with. The fence alignment block, in turn, is attached to a plywood base, which in turn is attached to the bottom of the fence.

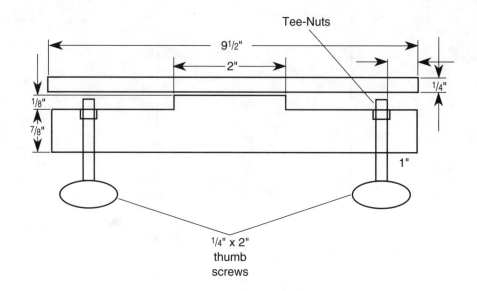

Tee-Nuts

9¹/₂"

2"

¹/₄"

¹/₈"

⁷/₈"

1"

¹/₄" x 2"
thumb
screws

Fence alignment block

The fence alignment block is a piece of 2×4 stock cut to 1½" × 1½" × 9½". It is then cut into the shape shown in the drawing below. Tee-nuts, or ordinary nuts epoxied in place, allow the thumb screws to contact with the wood facing, and allow you to square the fence to the table. The facing is cut from the same block and after you have cut the other shape and drilled the holes for the nuts or tee-nuts and the thumb screws, it is reattached to the other part using glue and 1" drywall screws.

Step 13

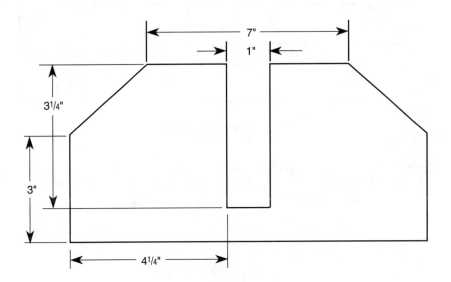

Fence alignment block base

Measure and cut the fence alignment block base from the Baltic birch plywood. The fence alignment block is attached to the base as shown in the drawing at the top of the next page. It absolutely must be square to the base. Use 1" drywall screws and glue to hold it in place.

Step 14

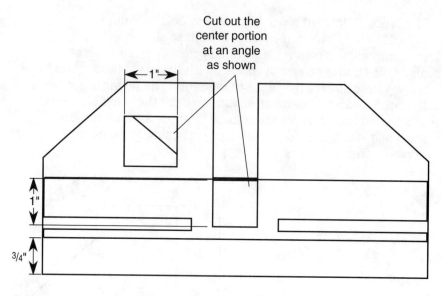

Cut out the center portion at an angle as shown

1"

1"

3/4"

Fence alignment block assembly

Step 15 Measure and cut all of the other fence pieces: the center board, plywood sides, end boards, and the cam and locking boards as shown below and on the next page.

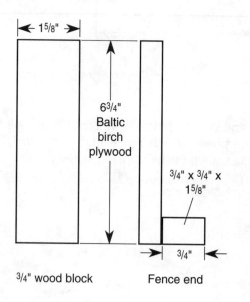

1⁵/₈"

6³/₄"
Baltic
birch
plywood

3/4" x 3/4" x
1⁵/₈"

3/4"

3/4" wood block

Fence end

196 Workshop accessories you can make

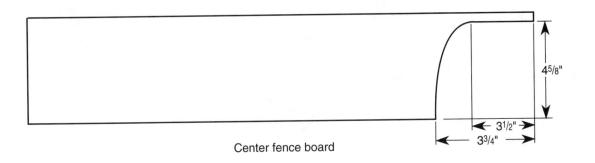

Center fence board

4⁵/₈" → $4^{5/8}"$

3¹/₂"

3³/₄"

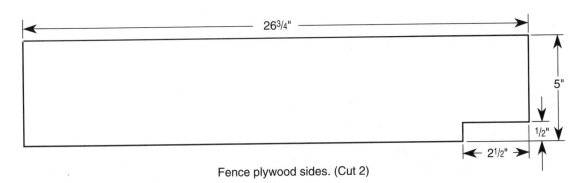

26³/₄"

5"

1/2"

2¹/₂"

Fence plywood sides. (Cut 2)

Combination table saw 197

Step 16 The drawings that are provided in this chapter for the end of the fence, the cam, and locking lever are shown full-size (see below and the next page). Since you are making your own version of this project, it is important that you allow for adjustments to your work. For example, if you are off by as little as ⅟₁₆" in the slot preparation, it is going to have a dramatic effect on the cam-locking action.

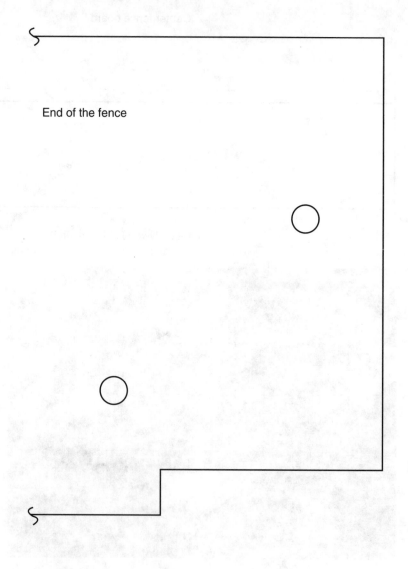

End of the fence

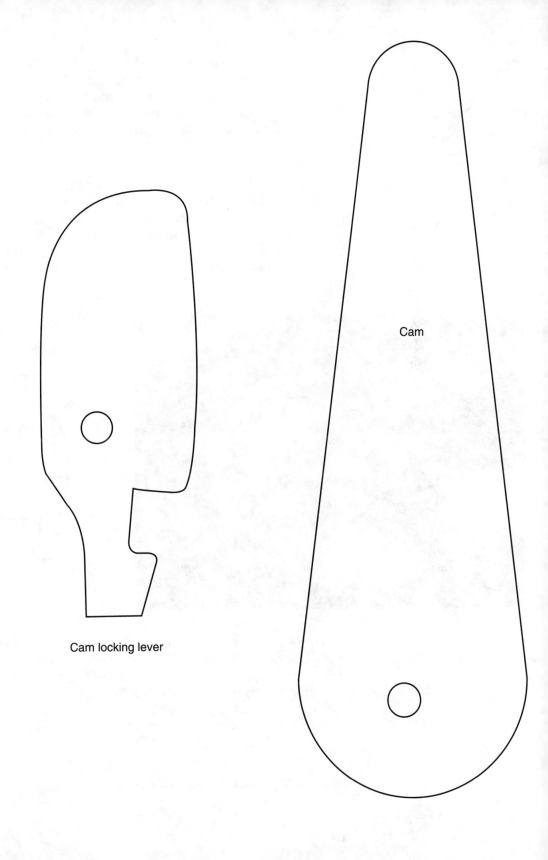

Cam locking lever

Cam

In short, what I am saying is you are going to have to go through a bit of trial and error before you get it right. The important thing is that when the fence is in the locked position, it must not move to the right or left. If you are even a little unsure, add a clamp to the fence.

Step 17   The cam and the locking mechanism are held in place with the use of pieces of ⅜" wood dowel 1¾" long. These are glued to the plywood sides of the assembly. The holes in the locking mechanism and the cam should be made slightly larger so that these items move freely when clamping the fence to the table top. The tip of the cam should be rough not smooth to work properly.

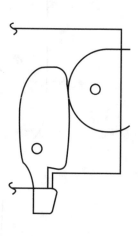

Assemble the cam and locking lever on the end of the fence using one side of the plywood and the center board only. When you are certain that the cam and locking lever are working correctly, add the second piece of side board and hold in place with drywall screws. Add the end boards shown at the bottom of page 189. The bottom of the end board should hang under the end of the table so that when the cam is activated, it pulls up snug against the table locking the fence in place.

The last step for this part of the project is to attach the **Step 18** polycarbonate material to the bottom of the circular saw. Since I do not know the kind of saw you plan to use, it is very difficult to give you exact directions. Basically what I did was take a piece of Lexan and center and square it on the saw. I cut out a center part that was large enough for the saw blade to drop down with the guard intact. I then widened the hole so that the saw could tilt up to a 45-degree angle. I then attached the saw to the polycarbonate using four recessed flat-head stove bolts.

Measure and cut the Baltic birch plywood pieces forming the **Step 19** two L-shaped locking devices that hold the saw firmly to the table. Attach the two L-shaped brackets as shown below, and clamp the saw to the underside of the table using flat-head stove bolts, countersunk, and wing nuts with lock washers.

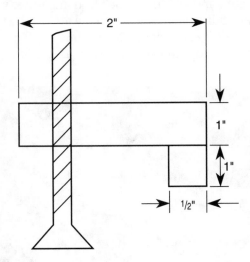

Make certain that the polycarbonate is flat and smooth with the tabletop and the screw heads are recessed so as to not interfere with work sliding across the tabletop as shown at the top of the next page.

Step 20 Next, measure and cut the Baltic birch and other wood pieces forming the sliding jig as shown below and at the top of the next page. This jig is designed to straddle the fence and has a toggle clamp to hold the work in place as it is fed into the blade.

202 Workshop accessories you can make

The sliding jig consists of two pieces of Baltic birch and two pieces of hardwood that essentially make it a U-shaped jig that fits over the fence so that it glides smoothly but has no excess movement right or left of the fence as shown on the next page.

The pieces are assembled as shown. The toggle lock is attached to the board marked A. Use glue and drywall screws to hold the assembly together.

Go find a board to cut!

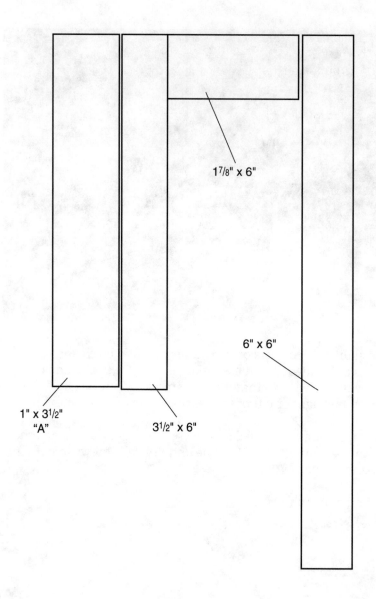

1⁷/₈" x 6"

6" x 6"

1" x 3¹/₂"
"A"

3¹/₂" x 6"

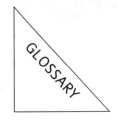

anchor bolt bolt set in concrete with its thread end projecting.

apex the top, particularly of a roof.

ark a building for animals, usually A-shaped.

bargeboards covering boards at the gable end of a roof.

battens strips of wood of light section, such as are used on a roof to hold down the covering.

bay a space or section in a building.

beam horizontal load-carrying member in any structure.

butt fit against another piece. The end of a log or post.

carriage bolt bolt with shallow domed head and square neck to grip wood. Also called coach bolt.

cladding the covering of boards that forms the outside of a wall.

clapboarding overlapping boards, usually tapered in section, and used as cladding.

coach bolt alternative name for carriage bolt.

coop small house for poultry.

dibbler, dibber tool for making holes in ground for planting bulbs etc.

drawknife broad cutting tool with handles at ends for cutting by pulling.

eaves   the angle between roof and wall. Overhang of roof over a wall. Never spelled without the s, even if there is only one.

exterior-grade plywood   weather-resistant plywood bonded with waterproof glue.

feather edge   wood tapered in section so one edge is thin.

foxiness   first signs of rot.

froe   knife-edge tool with lever handle for splitting wood.

gable   end of a roof, usually one with a ridge.

gusset   covering piece to make joint between two or more parts.

handed   made as a pair.

haft   a straight handle, as on a hammer.

hurdle   portable section of fence, often made like a gate.

hutch   house for small animals, such as rabbits.

jack   lifting device. Helping equipment such as boot jack.

jamb   upright side of doorway.

joist   a supporting beam, as in a floor.

kerf   the groove left when a saw cuts.

ledger   crosswise member, particularly on a door. Also called ledge.

lintel   support for a load over a doorway or other opening.

nominal   when applied to lumber, this is the sawn size. Wood finished by machine planing will have smaller sections.

paling   upright piece on a fence. Also called picket.

picket   alternative name for paling.

pilot hole   small hole drilled to check direction before enlarging to the required size.

pitch   slope of a roof. Distance between tops of a screw thread.

pop hole   hole in door or wall for poultry to pass through.

purlin   lengthwise support for roof covering, usually supported on rafters.

rabbet   recess in edge of wood, as in a picture frame. Also called *rebate*.

rafter   support for a roof.

rail   horizontal structural member.

ridge   the apex of a roof when made like an inverted V.

rive   to split wood deliberately.

roof truss   braced framework with rafters for supporting a roof.

season   to dry newly felled wood to an acceptable moisture level.

shake lengthwise, naturally formed crack in wood.

sheathing outside covering, such as cladding on a building.

shiplap boards cladding boards to be laid horizontally, with the upper edge of each one fitting into a rabbet in the one above.

siding the material used for cladding or sheathing.

sill projecting horizontal board, as at the bottom of a window, to shed water away from the wall below. Also spelled *cill*.

slat narrow strip of thin wood.

span distance, particularly width of a roofed building.

stable door door in two parts, so you can open the top part while the lower part remains closed. Not necessarily on a stable.

stud vertical support in a wall.

template (templet) wood cut to desired outline and used for marking shapes, particularly when they have to be repeated.

tie member under tension in a structure, as across a roof truss, where it prevents rafters spreading.

tines teeth, as in a rake.

tongue-and-groove boards prepared so a tongue on the edge of one piece fits in a groove in the edge of the next piece.

trellis strips of wood arranged across each other to form a pattern of diamond openings. Used for decoration or to support climbing plants.

triangulation dividing a framework into triangles, as when placing a member diagonally across a four-sided figure, so it keeps its shape.

truss framed support, as in a roof truss.

vent an arrangement in a roof or wall to provide ventilation.

waney edge the shape of the outside of a tree retained on the edge of a board that has not been squared.

weatherboarding cladding boards to be laid horizontally, tapered in the width so the thin edge of a lower board goes under the thicker edge of the board above.

wicket gate small gate intended only for pedestrians and usually covered with upright palings.

wind bracing diagonal bracing arranged in the roof between gable, trusses, and purlins to resist distorting loads in the roof due to strong winds.

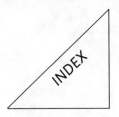

INDEX

Other Bestsellers of Related Interest

WOODWORKING FOR BEGINNERS—R.J. De Cristoforo

"R.J. De Cristoforo is the outstanding tool authority in the world." **—Popular Science**

Let a master craftsman guide you through your first steps to success in this practical guide. Stressing safety, it introduces the wide variety of hand tools used in woodworking and explains how to use them, as well as how not to use them. You'll take a look at handy power tools and discover how they can be adapted to perform different tasks. Plus, you'll find 25 easy-to-build, yet decorative and useful, items for the home or workshop, including a workbench, a sawhorse, a bookcase, a coffee table, a knife rack, and more. 272 pages, 350 illustrations. Book No. 4117, $15.95 paperback, $24.95 hardcover

FRAMES AND FRAMING: The Ultimate Illustrated How-to-Do-It-Guide—Gerald F. Laird and Louise Meiere Dunn, CPF

This illustrated step-by-step guide gives complete instructions and helpful illustrations on how to cut mats, choose materials, and achieve attractively framed art. Filled with photographs and eight pages of full color, this book shows why a frame's purpose is to enhance, support, and protect the artwork, and never call attention to itself. You can learn how to make a beautiful frame that complements artwork. 208 pages, 264 illustrations, 8 color pages. Book No. 2909, $14.95 paperback only

CARPENTRY & CONSTRUCTION—2nd Edition—Rex Miller and Glenn E. Baker

Tackle even the most ambitious construction projects on your own with the start-to-finish techniques outlined in this guide. Revised to include the latest home construction methods, materials, and equipment, it's an ideal on-the-site reference for any carpentry project. Clear instructions and more than 1,300 photographs and illustrations guide you step-by-step through the planning, building, or remodeling of a home. From planning and site preparation to interior finishing, you'll find it all here. 560 pages, 1,353 illustrations. Book No. 3678, $42.95 hardcover only

FENCES, DECKS, AND OTHER BACKYARD PROJECTS—3rd Edition—Dan Ramsey

Transform your backyard living space from the ordinary into the extraordinary with this fantastic idea book. Packed with step-by-step instructions and hundreds of illustrations, this updated guide shows you how to choose, design, prepare, build, and maintain all types beautiful fences, decks, and other outdoor structures. Veteran how-to author Dan Ramsey offers a veritable bonanza of backyard building ideas. 288 pages, over 300 illustrations. Book No. 4071, $14.95 paperback, $24.95 hardcover

THE TABLE SAW BOOK—R.J. De Cristoforo

"R.J. De Cristoforo is the outstanding tool authority in the world." **—Popular Science**

This book is a complete and practical approach to basic and advanced table saw functions. Detailed instructions and hundreds of illustrations are included for crosscuts, rips, miters, tapers, chamfers, dadoes, compound angles, and more. 352 pages, 500 illustrations. Book No. 2789, $16.95 paperback only

To Order Call Toll Free 1-800-822-8158
(24-hour telephone service available.)

or write to TAB Books, Blue Ridge Summit, PA 17294-0840.

Title	Product No.	Quantity	Price

☐ Check or money order made payable to TAB Books

Charge my ☐ VISA ☐ MasterCard ☐ American Express

Acct. No. _____ Exp. _____

Signature: _____

Name: _____

Address: _____

City: _____

State: _____ Zip: _____

Subtotal	$ _____
Postage and Handling ($3.00 in U.S., $5.00 outside U.S.)	$ _____
Add applicable state and local sales tax	$ _____
TOTAL	$ _____

TAB Books catalog free with purchase; otherwise send $1.00 in check or money order and receive $1.00 credit on your next purchase.

Orders outside U.S. must pay with international money in U.S. dollars drawn on a U.S. bank.

TAB Guarantee: If for any reason you are not satisfied with the book(s) you order, simply return it (them) within 15 days and receive a full refund.

BC